LAURA ASHLEY

Decorating CHILDREN'S ROOMS

LAURA ASHLEY
Decorating
CHILDREN'S ROOMS

CREATING FUN, PRACTICAL AND SAFE
SURROUNDINGS FOR YOUR CHILD

JOANNA COPESTICK

Special photography by Lucinda Symons

EBURY PRESS
LONDON

First published in 1996

1 3 5 7 9 10 8 6 4 2

First published in the United Kingdom in 1996 by Ebury Press
Random House, 20 Vauxhall Bridge Road, London SW1V 2SA

Random House Australia (Pty) Limited
20 Alfred Street, Milsons Point, Sydney, New South Wales 2061, Australia

Random House New Zealand Limited
18 Poland Road, Glenfield, Auckland 10, New Zealand

Random House South Africa (Pty) Limited
PO Box 337, Bergvlei, South Africa

Random House UK Limited Reg. No. 954009

A catalogue record for this book is available from the British Library.

ISBN 0 09 180774 3

Step-by-step text by Alison Wormleighton

Edited by Alison Wormleighton
Designed by Christine Wood
Special photography by Lucinda Symons
Styling by Lucy Elworthy
Illustrations by Kate Simunek

Printed and bound in Great Britain by Butler and Tanner Ltd, Frome, Somerset

Papers used by Ebury Press are natural recyclable products made from wood grown in
sustainable forests.

Contents

Introduction

The family and home were central to Laura Ashley's life. With four children, she had to give the decoration of nurseries and children's rooms a lot of thought, and the Victorian nursery was Laura Ashley's main source of inspiration. She wanted to re-create a traditional nursery that had been part of the house over generations and where successive children had played and enjoyed similar pastimes and hobbies. Many of the original Laura Ashley floral fabrics and wallpapers, such as those used in the little girl's pink bedroom on pages 82-3, were particularly suited to her nostalgic view.

The lifestyles of children today are continually changing and the designs of the Laura Ashley Mother & Child prints reflect this. A child's bedroom must be not only a practical and comfortable environment but also an inspiring place for creative play and learning. Wide pictorial borders or friezes have introduced many different themes to the collection. These themes have been carried through into fabrics and wallpapers to tell a complete story. Also part of the collection are fabrics and wallpapers with simple patterns such as colourful spots, watercoloured ginghams and painterly stripes. These coordinate with the rest of the collection, enabling you to create a truly original scheme for your child's bedroom. In this book the themes are traditional but most of the rooms have been decorated in a contemporary style, creating a colourful and jolly environment or a fantasy world.

This book includes a host of ideas for decorating and furnishing different children's rooms. With twenty-five step-by-step projects to help you do the decorating yourself – including some projects which require a child's helping hand – the book will help you not only to prepare for a new baby but also to provide for the needs of a growing child, from toddler to teenager.

Cheerful, busy borders can form the basis for a cohesive decorative scheme. Here, a sapphire blue gingham wallpaper makes a perfect backdrop for shades of mustard and chambray blue. The rag dolls and the building blocks are echoed in motifs in the fabric and in the wallpaper border, designed to look like a children's bookshelf.

CHAPTER ONE

Planning the Basics

Designing a room around the ever-changing whims of children can be quite a challenge, since youngsters cultivate tastes and preferences at a rate that would confound the most ardent and innovative home decorator. But by putting effort into creating a room reminiscent of a traditional and reassuring haven, crammed with interest and stimulation in terms of colour, pattern, toys and books, you can encourage successive generations to enjoy the simple pleasures of play.

A child's room is the one place in your house where you can be certain an adventurous decorating scheme will be successful. Walls that incorporate strong colour combinations, daring paper borders and brightly painted furniture and floorboards are just a few of the ways in which you can introduce vibrant colour and a lively sense of purpose into a scheme. You will also be encouraging your child to appreciate the delightful possibilities of colour, pattern and texture, giving him or her a headstart in becoming visually literate – a positive asset in a world where images rather than words dominate.

Fabric is the key in this feminine room. Bold, painterly harlequins create a quilt-like feeling for the bed cover and are juxtaposed with white and rose stripes on the bed curtains, while a colourful wallpaper border featuring ballet dancers is many a young girl's dream. A box bed such as this is both a cosy retreat and a means of saving space elsewhere in the room.

THE EVOLUTION OF THE NURSERY

The days when children were neither seen nor heard, but spent much of their youth cloistered in an attic nursery away from parents, are thankfully long gone. However, the nostalgic image of a Victorian nursery, decorated and equipped with traditional furnishings and toys, still serves as the quintessential blueprint to which many a new parent refers.

The evocative traditional nursery of Victorian times evolved towards the end of the 1800s, when people first began to devote some attention to the decorating and furnishing of

Colour, inspiration and a coordinated scheme of nursery rhyme characters prove that the modern-day nursery still incorporates the classic elements of comfort and storage but adds a touch of panache and adventure.

children's rooms – although they were not as colourful or inspirational as they are today. A typical Victorian nursery would usually have included a large toy-storage cupboard, a central round table for children to eat at and some rudimentary cooking facilities. Walls would have been covered with a simply decorated or deep-toned wallpaper, sealed with a glaze as a protective covering against sticky fingers. There may have been a few pictures on the walls. Furniture tended to be re-used from elsewhere in the house, often painted white to give it some uniformity.

Equipment specifically designed for the nursery would have included a wooden bassinet (movable crib), cradle and/or cot, a solid rocking horse (in more affluent households), a child-sized washstand, a willow-framed baby walker and a cane chair. Gradually, this room became a haven of work, rest and play, where children could spend hours at a time, playing, eating and sleeping with their siblings, in a microcosm of an adult's world.

Just as the plain decoration of the early nursery slowly succumbed to more ornate wallpaper, so toys developed from simple wooden shapes and rag dolls to encompass carefully crafted wooden Noah's arks complete with animals (deemed suitable as both toys and lessons in morality), painted building blocks, charming dolls' houses, finely decorated and dressed porcelain dolls and spinning tops. Books were always introduced to children in the nursery, too. The same basic components make a successful nursery today – the only concessions to modern needs being perhaps a dimmer switch and an alarm clock. Otherwise, the timeless appeal of wooden toys, heirloom furniture and simple furnishings endures.

In addition to the ever-popular traditional elements, modern-day children's rooms also need to perform a variety of functions while providing a stimulating, fun environment in which youngsters can realize their full potential. A child's room needs to fulfil the roles of a sleep place, play area, workroom and personal space. It must house a variety of toys, a computer,

music equipment, clothes, a seating area and a homework desk.

The main difference between a contemporary young person's room and the Victorian nursery is that today's child does not spend so much time in his or her own room. It is more of a personal place, somewhere to retreat to when they want to play, think, or escape a noisy family life. Nowadays, children share the whole of the house with their parents – especially the living room and the kitchen, which, if given a free hand, they may colonize completely with their belongings and, later on, friends.

PLANNING THE SPACE

The secret of making a child's room one that will be cherished for years to come is to build in a level of flexibility in your decoration, furniture and furnishings. This will allow for periodic changes in the room to reflect a child's growth and development. Planning the room with an eye on future needs is particularly useful if you want to avoid having to revamp the scheme too often. Once you have decided on the type and style of furniture, be it old country pine, painted and stencilled new wood, MDF (medium density fibreboard) or wood substitutes such as laminate, you can take a few risks when you come to address the decoration of walls and windows, furniture and floor.

Firstly, consider the size and shape of the room and decide how many children it might eventually house – this will affect the type of furniture you should plan to acquire over the

next few years. Obviously your decorating decisions will be based on the style of furniture you favour and whether you have one child or more, boys or girls, or both.

Shared bedrooms are often sensible options when space is at a premium or when siblings are quite close in age – youngsters soon learn to appreciate the comfort and security offered by a shared space. As they get older, though, it is important to provide each with an area of the room they can call their own, particularly once they enter the teenage years.

Check that there are enough power points in the room – initially for lights, and later on for equipment such as a computer, a television and a stereo system. You can never have too many power points.

Allocate space for clothes and toy storage. It is more flexible to provide freestanding toy storage, but you could build-in some wardrobe/cupboard space if there is an alcove in the room.

Decide whether there are any obvious architectural features which you could emphasize and enhance as focal points, such as fireplaces, alcoves or bay windows. The space inside an old, disused fireplace can be utilized for displaying or storing toys or a miniature table and chairs, while window seats placed inside a bay window and fitted with hinged lids provide additional storage space. Children love nooks and crannies in which they can hide, or create miniature worlds with their toys, so make the most of any awkward-shaped corners or built-in cupboards that may already exist in your home.

COLOURFUL WALLS AND FLOORS

All children adore bright colours and busy patterns, so seize the chance to be inventive. Create a bright, lively and fanciful scheme by using large expanses of rich, saturated colour on the walls, interspersed with vibrant paper borders, painted wooden panelling or striped freehand designs.

You could also try your hand at a simple mural. Decide on an image or scene, possibly based on the theme of the room, such as teddy bears or ducks, and transfer your image to the wall using graph paper.

Another way of making a dramatic colour statement is to divide the wall in half horizontally using two strongly contrasting colours, such as primrose yellow above and a luminous powder blue below. You can either separate the colours with a straight line ranged around the room, or try a more freehand approach and introduce a wavy line, a zigzag formation or a crenellated edge halfway up the wall. Simply mark out your chosen border with a pencil and steel rule, then apply masking tape to all edges before you apply the second colour. These are all simple but highly effective ways of introducing panels of strong colour into a room.

If your child becomes tired of any one border, you can conceal it by applying a paper border over it to mark the transition between colours, or simply change the colour above or below your dividing line. To further emphasize a colour scheme, paint freehand borders of colour around a favourite picture frame, or punctuate the walls with small display shelves painted in a similar or contrasting colour.

For children who are obsessed with drawing, fix a length of hardboard along the bottom edge of one or two walls and paint it with blackboard paint to provide a permanent drawing slate and an ever-changing focal point in the room. Alternatively, apply blackboard paint to the back of freestanding bookshelves as a way of dividing up the space in a room. You could create a reading area, using two bookshelves placed at right angles in the corner of the room to form walls and an "entrance". Furnish the corner with miniature wooden chairs, a small round table and a wicker basket for storing large picture books. Fix peg rails along the walls at dado height and suspend fabric or lightweight books from them using coloured string or raffia. What better way to encourage nursery readers? Or remove the books and transform the space into a make-believe shop, using the blackboard for drawings of the goods on sale – fruit and vegetables or clothes and toys.

Instead of covering up floorboards with wall-to-wall carpet, treat the floor as a blank canvas on which to paint decorative designs. Older children would love to help paint on a chequerboard pattern or chevron border in two or more colours. For babies and toddlers, try painting or stencilling simple motifs such as polkadots, wide and narrow stripes or farmyard animals. Warm up the room in winter with the addition of a generous-sized rag rug or a traditional painted floorcloth. Or turn the floor into a playground by painting on a hopscotch game or small chequerboard for draughts.

Other suitable floor coverings for children's rooms are natural coir, sisal or seagrass matting, which is hardwearing and durable. It is not so suited to crawling babies, however, as it can be rough on their knees. Cork tiles are a good choice, since they are relatively inexpensive, easy to clean and warm underfoot; they can be enhanced by the addition of a brightly coloured rug or floorcloth.

Try to keep a fair amount of floorspace uncluttered so that children have room to play, as well as a clear area for spreading out the contents of dolls' houses, baskets of small toys, large jigsaw puzzles or a collection of wooden building blocks.

Dots, stripes and nursery motifs combine in a jolly scheme based around the classic nursery colours of sapphire blue and poppy red. Pretty scalloped detailing on the roller blind, window seat cushions and chair cushion softens the edges and helps to draw the whole look together.

DECORATING WITH FABRIC

Fabric is a key element for providing pattern and colour in children's rooms. If you don't want to adorn a baby's nursery in swathes of elaborate chintz – which will quickly pall when your child, aged three years, becomes a whirlwind of energy, desperate to assume the attributes of a miniature adult – select a quite grown-up fabric, such as a checked, striped or simple floral design, as a starting point. Use an age-related fabric, such as a novelty print of ducks, teddy bears, circus clowns or nursery-rhyme characters for cushions, duvet covers, roller blinds or draped swags. That way you will only have to replace the smaller items every few years, while the main curtains, upholstery, scatter cushions and bedlinen can remain the same for quite a while.

Often it is the small decorative details of a room that linger in children's minds long after they have outgrown their first bedroom. Use fabric for making drawstring bags of varying sizes and hang them on a peg rail to store small toys, bricks, hair bands or ribbons and general clutter. Or make charming nightdress or pyjama bags out of pretty fabric in the shape of animals. Line generous-sized wicker baskets with gingham fabric for versatile toy storage. On open shelves, use fabric to make a tie blind which serves the dual purpose of keeping out the dust and covering up the toys so that they do not lose their novelty value.

Any fabric scraps from family heirlooms such as silk evening gowns or old patchwork quilts can be worked up into a bed quilt, wall hanging or pyjama bag. Or make soft toys in simple animal shapes using floral, spotted or plain fabric remnants.

Girls, no matter how equality-conscious their parents may be, all seem to go through a "Pink Phase", which can last for several years. During this time they yearn for a romantic pink haven in which to play their fairy-tale games, so be prepared to create a corona emblazoned with draped pink organza or acquire some lace-trimmed bedlinen. See page 83 for a pink room fit for a would-be princess.

There is no escaping the differences in behaviour between girls and boys. It is the same process that drives some boys, despite not being allowed to play with toy weapons, to create swords and rapiers from scrap pieces of cardboard and newspaper. Their heart's desire would be a room decked out as a pirate's cave or a sailboat, so, likewise, steel yourself for hours spent inserting eyelets into lengths of yacht canvas, lashing mock sails to bedposts or decorating treasure chests.

Of course, there is no need to be so comprehensively indulgent when your child hits one of these phases. A generously draped bed canopy over a young girl's bed has been known to satisfy her romantic nature, while a temporary box of treasure and a passable cardboard imitation of a ship and a Jolly Roger flag could suffice for a boy.

Yet there is something incredibly satisfying about creating a complete scheme for a child's room. The distinct periods of childhood pass so quickly, and it is always the handmade beds and

playhouses built over a weekend, the lovingly sewn quilts and dolls' house furnishings, or the personally stencilled toy boxes that children remember well into adulthood, and carry with them as talismans of their parents' affection.

These circus-style cabinas add a touch of humour to cowslip stripe walls and curtains. More stripes form tie-up blinds on each cabina, while clowns adorn the wallpaper border and other small-scale detailing, making the circus theme complete. The buttoned heading on the curtains is echoed in the colour of the drawer knobs.

FURNITURE, STORAGE AND DISPLAY

In any bedroom, the bed is the most important piece of furniture you will acquire, and this is even more the case in children's rooms, as you want them to sleep comfortably and securely at night, with proper support for their backs.

In the early years, once a cot has been outgrown, at around the age of two, you should be able to combine the aesthetic with the practical and choose a bed to suit your circumstances. Antique box beds are perfect for the younger child as the sides are raised slightly at either end, preventing them from falling out in the night. Slot wicker baskets under the bed base for extra storage. Alternatively, a new pine single bed often comes complete with a generous-sized drawer on castors.

A pretty draped four-poster bed is the centrepiece of a room decorated in simple pink and cream country florals. Delightfully feminine and irresistibly timeless, this rustic haven, with plum detailing and simple frills, is a fairy tale come true for girls of all ages.

The most versatile of all beds are bunks and high-level designs, whose components can be rearranged to form under-bed desks or shelves. Eminently practical and flexible, these components can be painted and distressed to make them look more appealing and in keeping with a traditional decorative scheme.

Beds also offer a good chance to reflect your chosen decorative theme with bedlinen. Additional pillows, bolsters or quilts in a style chosen by the children or parents can help unify or distinguish a particular theme. When pre-school children are going through the phase of wanting gaudy cartoon characters splashed over every movable object, it is usually acceptable to acquiesce on a couple of items, such as the pillowcase or duvet cover, on the understanding that a pretty bed cover adorns the bed for most of the day. Alternatively, stand your ground on bedlinen, but be supremely indulgent when it comes to pyjamas, nightdresses and slippers!

Children's clothes and toys are often appealing decorative objects in their own right, so capitalize on this by showing them off to their full effect. Display baby clothes on small hangers suspended from peg rails, and intersperse them with rows of hats and hairbands or bags and puppets. Change the display regularly so that a baby has a varied view from the cot.

For all the other clothes and bedlinen, the most useful pieces of furniture are a chest of drawers and a wardrobe or cupboard. A sturdy old pine chest will see a child right through from infancy to adulthood. Freestanding wardrobes and cupboards are more versatile than built-in ones if you want to alter the room's layout when more children come along, or if you are marking the transition from one phase of childhood to the next. A row of built-in cupboards does make maximum use of space, however, and you can always consider replacing or painting the doors to ring the changes.

Painted furniture is a real asset in children's rooms. Antique chests of drawers and book-shelves that have seen better days can be transformed with two coats of water-based paint in contrasting colours, their surfaces gently aged. For extra decoration, apply découpaged motifs or simple stencils to the finished pieces. For examples of this type of decoration on cupboards, furniture and even a fireplace, see our Little Princess's Bedroom, page 84.

The more interesting and varied you can make the storage in a child's room, the more inclined they will be to help tidy up. It is much more appealing to help pile clothes into a colourful basket or a painted toy box than to cram objects into a battered cupboard or rows of junk-filled open shelves. Colourful baskets are also great for offsetting garish plastic toys.

Screens are another useful way of disguising cluttered corners or partitioning a room when two children are sharing the same space. Use them to demarcate specific areas or as decorative objects in their own right. Paint them with blackboard paint, or coat them with a cork surface and use them as freestanding pinboards. Alternatively, cover them with fabric that matches the curtains and upholstery. You can also attach small hooks to the screens for displaying bags or for storing dressing-up clothes, creating an instant dressing room.

GETTING THE LIGHT RIGHT

Lighting is often ignored until the last moment when people are planning to decorate a room, but it is vitally important to get it right. Children's rooms are no exception, and they call for a greater degree of flexibility and safety than other rooms in the house.

A dimmer switch for the main overhead light is the first requirement. From the nursery years onwards, a dimmer is invaluable for providing just enough light to feed by, or if you want to check that children are tucked up nicely and fast asleep when you go to bed yourself.

Provide a wall-mounted lamp or bedside light for older children to read by, but do not leave any trailing flexes visible. Lampshades, available in a wide variety of styles and colours for lamps and overhead pendant lights, are something children will enjoy choosing themselves. Plug-in nightlights are useful for nurseries, or for children who don't like complete darkness.

TRADITIONAL TOYS

Painted wooden toys will last a lifetime, and offer a reassuring, nostalgic familiarity that can never be provided by mass-produced playthings. Nothing can match the timeless elegance of a polished and painted wooden rocking horse, a push-along puddleduck, a painted revolving roundabout, a set of weathered building blocks or a well-loved dolls' house, whose smooth, worn surfaces hint at the busy, happy hours of an earlier generation.

Children undoubtedly respond to bright primary colours, but they also appreciate natural textures, and the tactile qualities of wood and fabric surpass plastic every time. Painted wooden toys that can be handed down the generations make superb adornments for a child's room, so use them as decoration in their own right. Create a still life of wooden toys and soft rag dolls on a miniature wicker sofa, or line them up, two by two, atop a painted wall cupboard.

Another cherished possession of many children is the dressing-up box. Painted, stained, varnished or stencilled, it is a treasure chest of props and clothes, hats and wraps, snakes and magic wands. The importance of creative play in a child's development is a favourite theme of child psychologists. Recent research suggests that an imaginative child is more likely to be receptive to learning and more able to take a balanced view of life's ups and downs.

Psychology apart, there is nothing quite so captivating as the sight of young children immersed in imaginative play. The sheer delight they take in transforming everyday objects into ever more complex and ornate props for their fantasy worlds is truly fascinating. Adults may be inspired by watching the way in which a bed, its duvet, blankets and cushions can be conjured into glorious galleons or grandiose turreted castles. This kind of timeless make-believe is

fun, free and educational: the carpet might look like a utilitarian floor covering to you, but to children at play it becomes, with the addition of a few sofa cushions, a treacherous swamp inhabited by dangerous crocodiles. Only in a room in which children feel totally secure and comfortable can these forays into the imagination take place. Swallows and Amazons was never more vivid.

Encourage imaginative play by providing a few basic props such as floor cushions, discarded

This quintessential Victorian nursery incorporates subtle rose-coloured fabric at the window and on the upholstery. A simple painted floor and a traditional rug are the perfect complement for traditional toys.

sheets with eyeholes cut out of them for ghost and monster games, and a selection of hats for quick character changes. Don't forget that even everyday items like brooms, buckets, mops and cardboard boxes can be put to good use by the would-be avenging swashbuckler or by the beautiful princess in peril.

CHAPTER TWO

Room for Change

When you are planning a nursery for a new baby, it's difficult to think beyond the infant's immediate needs. The fact that a desk will be necessary at some remote time in the future seems hardly relevant when nappy-changing and feeding are dominating life.

Nevertheless, it's worth trying to think in the long-term. A little planning will allow you to adapt the room to the child's changing needs and interests without having to redecorate and refurnish completely. Not only is this approach more practical, but it will help maintain continuity through the years.

Wall and window treatments do not necessarily have to have a nursery motif to look appropriate for a baby. Instead, you can choose a design with a fairly broad appeal, then introduce the nursery element with pictures and accessories. Similarly, furniture can be adapted to different purposes over the years, as in the room featured on the following pages. It is shown in three guises: the first (left) is a nursery; the second (on page 27 and also shown in more detail in Chapter Four) is for a pre-school child; and the third (on pages 28–9) is a teenager's room. The basics have remained the same, yet each room is both functional and hugely appealing.

The first stage of our "transition room" shows a nursery configuration. The wallpaper border, with its Owl and the Pussycat theme, provided the starting point for the room. A thin strip of the border is repeated on the storage unit, while chambray, cowslip and apple fabrics in checks and florals sit happily alongside colourwash striped wallpaper. The generously draped Moses basket coordinates with the dresser unit, and the easy chair will appeal to all ages.

INFANCY

The delightful sunny scheme of chambray blue and cowslip yellow shown on pages 20–1 would suit either a girl or a boy. Checked curtains and striped wallpaper combine well with stencilled stars and moons taken from the wallpaper border. The shelves of the storage unit are lined with checked fabric, and a flat curtain covers the lower shelves; both fabrics tone with florals used elsewhere in the room.

The multi-purpose storage unit provides endlessly flexible accommodation for baby clothes and toiletries, as well as a nappy-changing area. Everything is at hand when the fold-down changing table is in use.

STORAGE UNIT

The freestanding storage unit, which serves as both a dresser and a changing table, consists of a shelf unit sitting on a base, both constructed from 2.5cm (1in) thick timber. The shelves on the base are made from slats fixed to horizontal supports. A piece of thick wooden dowelling inserted through holes drilled in the frame provides hanging space for a baby's clothes. The dowelling extends beyond the shelves to act as a place to hang a handmade mobile (see page 26). The entire piece can be adjusted over the years to provide a variety of uses – as storage, work space and hobby area (see page 31).

A changing table projects about 75cm (30in) at the side of the unit and has a timber support underneath. (Even though there is a rim around the edge, remember that a baby should never be left unattended on a changing table, however briefly, because of the risk of falling off.) The table can be folded down out of the way when not in use.

Enhance the finished unit by lining the backs of the shelves on the top half with fabric, wallpaper or wrapping paper. Decorate the rim with a narrow border; the one shown here was a detail taken from the Owl and the Pussycat wallpaper border that runs around the room at chair rail height. A coordinating fabric panel on the base unit conceals a useful storage area and softens the lines of the dresser. These finishing touches can all be altered at any time to change the look of the room.

LAYETTE BASKET

A basket like the one on the storage unit (opposite), with a pretty, washable lining, is indispensable in a nursery, and can be used in later years for storing all kinds of items.

YOU WILL NEED

FABRIC
MATCHING SEWING THREAD
LIGHTWEIGHT WADDING

1 Make a pattern and cut out fabric and wadding for the base and sides, as directed for the Moses Basket Lining (page 44, step 1), but adding only 1.25cm (½in) all around for seam allowances.

2 Place the wadding on the wrong side of one fabric piece for each side pattern; tack in place. Our lining is not quilted but you can quilt it if you wish (see page 45, Basket Lining step 2).

3 With right sides together, join both ends of the padded side pieces to form a ring, taking a 1.25cm (½in) seam. Trim away the wadding in the seam allowances. Repeat for the unpadded fabric pieces.

4 Cut out 7.5cm (3in) wide strips for the frill and join the ends to make a single continuous strip that is double the distance around the rim. (Our fabric makes the frill appear to be cut on the bias, but it is cut on the straight grain.) Fold it in half lengthwise, wrong sides together; press and tack along the long raw edge. Arrange the folded strip into 1.25cm (½in) knife pleats every 4.5cm (1¾in) or so. Tack along the raw edge of the frill.

5 Make four pairs of ties by cutting eight 5cm (2in) wide fabric strips on the straight grain; they should be long enough to tie in bows around the basket handles. Fold each in half lengthwise, right sides together, and stitch down the long edge, taking a 6mm (¼in) seam, and then stitch across one end at an angle. Trim the corners, turn right side out and press.

6 Position the pleated frill along the top edge of the padded ring, right sides together and raw edges even; tack in place. Place two ties, one over the other, on top of the frill, with raw edges even, positioning them on one side of the handle. Do the same with two more on the other side of the handle. Repeat for the handle at the other end of the ring.

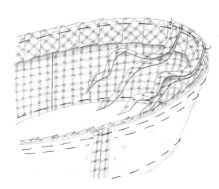

7 Lay the other ring on top, right sides together, and stitch around the top edge, taking a 1.25cm (½in) seam, and sandwiching in the frill and the ties. Trim seam, clip curves and trim away the wadding within the seam allowances. Turn right side out. Press, then tack the layers together along the lower edge.

8 Join the lower edge of the ring to the base (see page 45, Basket Lining step 4). Place the lining in the basket, and tie to the handles.

MOSES BASKET SKIRT AND CANOPY

A pleated skirt covers the stand of this Moses basket. The box pleats are arranged so that the checked bands of the fabric fall inside the pleats. The basket lining is made from the coordinating check fabric and trimmed with a plain fabric that picks out the blue found in the fabrics and elsewhere in the room. Above the basket a simple voile canopy is suspended from a wall-mounted pole. (This canopy should not be used when a baby is old enough to pull on it.)

YOU WILL NEED

FOR SKIRT AND QUILT
FLORAL FABRIC FOR SKIRT AND QUILT
CHECKED FABRIC FOR BASKET LINING AND FRILL ON QUILT
PLAIN FABRIC FOR TRIM
MATCHING SEWING THREAD
MEDIUM-WEIGHT WADDING

FOR CANOPY
BLOCK OF WOOD 1.25CM (½IN) THICK AND ABOUT 10CM (4IN) SQUARE
25CM (10IN) LENGTH OF WOODEN DOWELLING
VOILE OR MUSLIN
MATCHING SEWING THREAD

Skirt and quilt

1 From the checked fabric, make the lining as for the Layette Basket (page 23), steps 1–3.

2 Measure the distance from the top of the basket to the floor. Cut pieces of fabric to this length plus 4.5cm (1¾in) and join together at the sides until you have a ring measuring twice the distance around the basket. Press under 6mm (¼in) and then 2.5cm (1in) on the lower edge, and stitch. Arrange the fabric in equal box pleats so that the ring fits exactly around the top of

the basket. If you are using the fabric we used, the checked bands should fall inside the pleats. Tack all around.

3 Cut 7.5cm (3in) wide strips of plain fabric on the bias and join the ends (page 89, step 4) to form a continuous ring long enough to fit around the top of the pleated skirt. Lay it on the top of the basket and mark where the handles will be. Make a giant bound buttonhole for each handle.

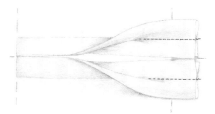

4 With right sides together, sew one edge of the trim to the top of the pleated skirt, and the other to the top of the padded lining. Complete as for the Layette Basket (page 23), steps 7–8, slotting the buttonholes over the

handles rather than tying the lining in place as for the Layette Basket.

5 Make the quilt from the floral fabric, as for the quilt on page 45, inserting a wide checked frill in the outer seam.

Canopy

1 Cut a 1.25cm (½in) thick block of wood into the shape shown. Drill a hole in it the same diameter as, or slightly less than, the dowelling. Screw the block to the wall about 1.8m (6ft) above floor level, using several screws. Shave the end of the dowel if necessary so it will fit tightly into the hole in the wood block.

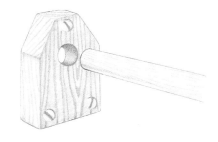

2 Cut a 4.3m (14ft) length of voile and hem the ends. (Using the full width of fabric eliminates the need for hems on the side edges.) Fold in half crosswise, right sides together, and stitch 1.25 (½in) from the fold to form a casing. Turn over, slot the dowel through the casing and drape around the basket.

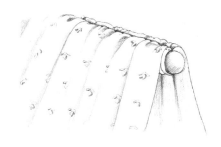

MOBILE

All the elements of this delightful fabric mobile are taken from the Owl and the Pussycat rhyme that appears on the wallpaper border: the owl's guitar, the "honey and plenty of money, wrapped up in a five-pound note", the stars they looked up to, the moon whose light they danced by, and especially the ring that enabled the pair to marry after sailing away for a year and a day.

YOU WILL NEED

2 PLASTIC-COATED WIRE COATHANGERS

THICK COTTON THREAD

FABRIC FOR COVERING HANGER

FELT FOR SHAPES

MATCHING SEWING THREAD

CHECKED GINGHAM FOR HONEYPOT

CORD FOR HONEYPOT

WADDING

SMALL COINS, TO USE AS WEIGHTS

1 Squeeze the top and bottom of each coat hanger together. Insert one hanger through the other with the two hooks together and twist the hangers into a four-pointed star. Wrap thick cotton thread around the centre.

2 Cut five 7.5cm (3in) wide strips of fabric, each 1½ times the length of an "arm" of the star. Fold in half lengthwise, right sides together, and stitch along the long edge and across one end. Turn right side out. Run a gathering thread along the length of each and pull up the threads. Encase the arms and also the hook in these ruched fabric tubes. Turn under the raw ends and hand sew the tubes together at the centre.

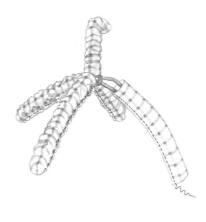

3 Cut out two shapes from the felt for each item. Machine stitch the smaller shapes onto each side. Machine stitch the guitar strings and fret in brown, and zigzag stitch the numeral "5" on the five-pound note. Stitch the two layers of each together around the edges, inserting a little wadding between the layers first. For the stars and guitar you could also insert a small coin as a weight. For the honeypot, add a gingham lid, trimmed with cord.

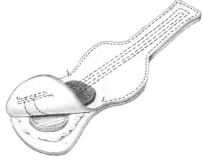

4 Suspend the felt pieces from the arms of the star with thick cotton thread, adjusting the lengths of the thread and the positions of the pieces so that the mobile looks balanced. If you want the mobile to move a lot, the lengths of string will need to be longer than those in the photograph.

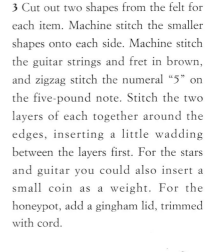

PRE-SCHOOL

When adapting the nursery to suit a pre-school child, the wallpaper, the stencilled stars and moons and the checked curtains can all stay as they are, and the storage unit can now be used for keeping toys tidy. A cot or a bed replaces the original Moses basket or crib, and the fabric that was chosen for the Moses basket and nursery dresser is suitable for a duvet cover and pillowcase. The wallpaper border that appeared at chair rail height in the nursery also features again, around the bottom of the bed this time.

Space has been left on the floor for lots of toys and for a foldaway playhouse, which is an ideal plaything for children of this age. Foldaway items allow you to clear the decks at the end of a day's play so that the toys do not lose their novelty value.

Any additional storage requirements can be accommodated by adding a fabric-covered cabina (see page 56). One of the advantages of this sort of storage is that it provides another opportunity to introduce fabric, which can be changed if desired when the child is older. (For more about this room, see page 52.)

In the second stage of our "transition room", the former nursery has been adapted for a pre-school child. The basics – wallpaper and stencilled frieze, curtains and flooring – are still the same, but a fun four-poster bed now has pride of place. The entire room is described in detail and illustrated on pages 52-7.

THE TEENS

When a tiny baby has become an active teenager, with study, relaxation and entertaining as the main priorities, the room is again easily adapted to a new age group. The original dresser storage unit now becomes a desk, providing a quiet and useful study area.

The wallpaper and curtains remain, but new soft furnishings have been created for the full-size bed, for a mattress used as a low day bed and for soft, squashy scatter cushions. Scraps of the existing fabrics have been incorporated in an oversized bedspread made from a toning blue fabric and edged in a wide border of ticking stripes. They help to unite the existing decor and the new approach. The cushions have a variety of borders and edgings, while the day bed is draped in a patchwork quilt of florals and checks. The original dressing-up box of several years ago is now an impromptu coffee table, housing books and magazines.

The atmosphere of the room is totally different from that of the nursery on pages 20–1, yet many of the original features are still in evidence. Careful planning of a child's room at the outset can pay dividends for years to come. Your teenager may also be secretly pleased that some vestigial elements of childhood remain.

A colourful retreat, this chambray blue, cowslip yellow and apple green room – the third stage of our "transition room" – is both comfortable and inspiring for a busy teenager. With plenty of room to relax with friends, as well as a comfortable worktop, desk and ample space for a pinboard which keeps the wall clear, emphasis is placed on the dramatic combination of checks and stripes in the three main colours.

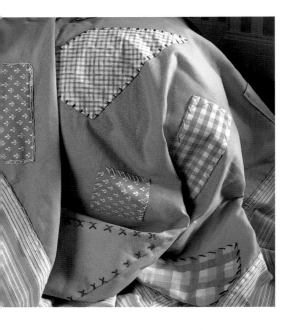

APPLIQUÉD PATCH BEDSPREAD

The patches on this upbeat bedspread are not pieced but appliquéd onto the background fabric. Cut bold patches in a range of shapes, sizes and fabrics, and appliqué them by turning under a narrow hem then hand sewing all around each edge. The large embroidery stitches used around the edges of the patches are in keeping with the bold design. Blanket stitch worked along the inner edge of the striped border helps to frame the patches. This is a project an artistic teenager might like to help with.

CUSHIONS

Piles of cushions are often considered essential in a teenager's room. Make them from fabrics used for the other soft furnishings, and ring the changes with the trim. The measurements given here are for 60cm (24in) square cushions, but they can be adjusted easily.

YOU WILL NEED

FABRIC

MATCHING THREAD

PIPING CORD AND BIAS BINDING IN
CONTRAST FABRIC, FOR PIPED CUSHION

COVERED BUTTONS, FOR BUTTONED
CUSHION

60CM (24IN) CUSHION PADS

Flanged cushion

1 For a cushion with a 10cm (4in) flange all around, cut a 63.5 x 63.5cm (25 x 25in) square, one 63.5 x 79cm (25 x 31in) rectangle and four 84 x 23cm (33 x 9in) strips of fabric. Cut the rectangle in half crosswise and turn under 6mm (¼in) then 2.5cm (1in) on the cut edge of both halves.

2 With *wrong* sides together and raw edges even, pin the back pieces to the front piece, overlapping the hemmed edges at the back to create an opening. Tack all around.

3 Press under 1.25cm (½in) on one long edge of each strip. With right sides together, stitch the other edge of each strip to the tacked edges of the fabric squares, taking a 1.25cm (½in) seam and stopping at the seamlines of the adjacent edges. Mitre the corners as shown. Turn each strip to the other side, pin the folded edge along the seamline and stitch along the seamline. Press. Insert the cushion pad through the opening in the back.

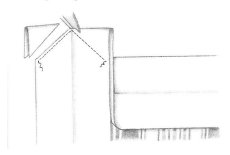

Buttoned cushion

1 Cut a 63.5 x 79cm (25 x 31in) rectangle for the front and a 63.5 x 63.5cm (25 x 25in) square for the back. Mark a line 15cm (6in) in from one short edge of the rectangle, and cut along this line.

2 Turn under 6mm (¼in) and then 2.5cm (1in) on the cut edges of the two front pieces, and make button-holes in the narrower piece.

3 Place the front and back pieces with right sides together, raw edges even and the hemmed edges overlapping so that the narrower front piece is next to the back piece. Stitch a 1.25cm (½in) seam around all four sides. Trim the corners and turn right side out. Sew covered buttons onto the wider front piece, beneath the buttonholes.

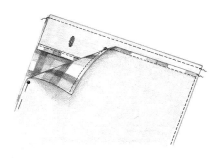

Piped cushion

Make an opening in the back as for the flanged cushion, but join the front and back with *right* sides together, inserting piping in the seam (see page 89, step 5). To make bias binding for the piping, see page 89, step 4.

STORAGE UNIT

The baby's dresser (page 22) is easily transformed into a study area with plenty of accessible storage. The fold-down table has been turned over so that it can be used as a desk; the rim that was on the changing table is now part of the decorative edging. The curtain panel that was on the base unit has been removed, revealing the slatted shelves, and the original fabric backing on the top unit has been replaced with zappy wrapping paper. Providing capacious but accessible storage, as well as a good-sized table top, the unit is as invaluable in a teenager's room as in that of a newborn babe.

CHAPTER THREE

The Nursery Years

A few centuries ago, nursery folklore demanded that a newborn baby be held aloft as soon as it was born, to ensure that it would do well and rise in the world. These days, the uplifting effect comes from a more practical and long-lasting source. A colourful, stimulating environment in which to spend time and play is now recognized as a prerequisite for a happy, healthy child. As a result, the decoration and planning of a first nursery has become a priority.

The notion of a traditional nursery, with its draped wooden crib, pristine white bedding and lovingly sewn quilts, is tremendously appealing. The magical presence of a peacefully sleeping baby never fails to touch all generations as they marvel over its delicate features and tiny fingers.

Harness some of the wonder of a new baby by making the nursery a place where the new family member can thrive and develop in surroundings which inspire and delight. Fill it with special family heirlooms such as hand-embroidered birth samplers and weathered wooden perambulators, treasured teddy bears or old blanket boxes and simple soft toys. Such timeless items will easily make the transition from one period of childhood to the next.

Our Ducks Nursery (see page 39) features a modern interpretation of traditional animal motifs. Ducks and the colour yellow are both classic choices for a nursery because they suit boys *and* girls. Yellow Canasta checked curtains are pinned back with a yellow tieback and finished off with a blue gingham covered button. The gingham is echoed in the wall hanging.

CHOOSING THE SITE

Try to site a nursery at the back of the home, away from street noise, and preferably in a room that receives a fair amount of natural light during the day – south-facing is ideal.

When choosing which room of the house to devote to the nursery, it isn't always entirely practical to do as the Victorians did and select the smallest box room at the top of the house. In the first year of your baby's life, you will be backwards and forwards to the nursery countless times, and the rest of the time listening out for the baby, so try not to have too much distance between it and your bedroom.

Babies grow so quickly that by the age of about two, a child will require a full-size single bed, additional toy and clothes storage and a clear floor space for playing. By thinking ahead at the very beginning you should be able to work out which will be the most suitable room for adapting from a cute, minimally furnished nursery, to an overladen toy store, to a place for friends to sleep over, to a teenage den.

It may be worth siting the nursery in the smallest bedroom if it is next to an existing bedroom. You could then consider knocking the two rooms into one when the baby is old enough to share a room with an older sibling. Alternatively, think about devoting a larger bedroom (yours perhaps) to a room that will double up as bedroom and playroom for years to come, thereby keeping space downstairs free for the grown-ups.

CREATING A NURSERY

The decorating and equipping of a nursery is an exciting departure into the hitherto mysterious world of layettes, musical mobiles and wallpaper borders, as well as an important chance to prepare yourself for a new way of life.

With the imminent arrival of a new baby, particularly the first one, there is a strong temptation to create a special room festooned in yards of soft-coloured delicate fabrics, with every available surface emblazoned with stencilled motifs. While such a tailor-made room is idyllic for a baby up to 12 months old, it quickly becomes inappropriate thereafter. A little restraint and a careful use of colour, fabric and furniture at an early stage can enable you to lay the decorative foundations of a room which has to evolve through several different stages of childhood.

Decorating a nursery provides a rare opportunity to plan and style a room from scratch as well as a chance to be more adventurous with colour and pattern than you might be in a formal living room or in a much-viewed kitchen. You can decide for yourself exactly what colours to use, choose very specific fabrics and unleash your artistic yearnings by decorating old chests of drawers or creating cot quilts and wall hangings.

Whether you settle on a cohesive scheme in which coordinating fabrics appear on curtains, upholstery, lampshades and accessories, or an eclectic mix of colours and patterns, there are a few basic guidelines to make your life easier when planning the decor.

DECORATING

Very often it is the window treatment that triggers off ideas for how to use fabric elsewhere in the room. A simple blind calls for a simple cot duvet, while a curtain pelmet and tiebacks could suggest a cot canopy or bed corona in another part of the room. Equally, plain, interlined pencil pleat curtains in a beautiful fabric offer simple, classic comfort and warmth.

Wallpaper borders are often good starting points for decorative schemes too. They usually incorporate a wide range of colours, any of which can be picked out and emphasized in wall colour, curtain fabric and soft furnishings. A bold border could be echoed with equally bold cushions in the dominant colour but toned down with simple checked curtains. Similarly, checked curtains could be contrasted with striped or spotted designs in the same colours used on small-scale accessories such as floor cushions and laundry bags. Mixing quite different fabrics in this way can be very successful and create surprising contrasts.

The nursery is the perfect chance to use animal motifs, which are nearly as popular with adults as with children. Themes such as the circus, nursery rhymes, teddy bears, numbers and the alphabet also have a timeless appeal.

A predominately pink or blue nursery is fine if you know in advance the sex of your child, or if you are prepared to postpone decorating the nursery till after the birth. Specifically feminine and masculine rooms can be created not just with colour but also with fabric – florals for girls and stripes for boys.

A procession of white farmyard ducks in a field of yellow narcissi makes a beautiful wallpaper border, especially painted in watercolours. The border was the starting point for the scheme for the Ducks Nursery (page 39).

Many nurseries, or course, are decorated before the baby's sex is known. Checks are a popular design for both boys and girls and work well with the "unisex" colours of green, yellow and red. Our simple yellow Ducks Nursery (pages 32–3) with checked curtains and a duck-motif wallpaper border (page 35) suits baby boys and girls. The classic nursery combination of green and yellow or blue and yellow also works for either sex. You can always add small accessories such as mobiles and posters in a defining colour if you wish. Another option is to paint the walls white or buttermilk and choose a wallpaper border, but leave the curtains or blinds and cot linen until after the baby's arrival.

Since babies spend quite a lot of time in their cots, consider painting small motifs – stars and moons or simple shapes – onto the ceiling. Or use a strong colour on the ceiling if the room is quite a good size. (Avoid deep colours in a small or low-ceilinged room, as it will make it seem even smaller.)

Floorboards look pretty stencilled with simple flowers or geometric shapes, or simply colour-washed in white or bright colours. Set them off with a large rag rug in the centre.

Although it is tempting to use ruffled or fussy curtains at the windows, often a more restrained look works better – and is easier to adapt later on. Try ungathered lengths of fabric lashed to metal or wooden poles by means of punched eyelets and thick jute rope, or simple Roman or roller blinds embellished with contrasting plain fabric edges or pulls.

EQUIPPING A NURSERY

Regardless of the style of decor you are planning, there is a certain amount of essential equipment for which you will need to find space (see opposite). The ideal nursery will be large enough to house a single bed eventually. It should have a decent-sized window and adequate heating and lighting. If possible, it should include a sink and a storage unit, which is invaluable at nighttime during the months of frequent nappy-changing.

Essential furniture includes a crib or cot and adequate storage. Built-in cupboards are useful for storing clothes, nappies and creams and spare towels and bedding, while babies' clothes are easily stored in drawers or on shelves.

A nappy-changing area will save backache if you are constantly bending down on the floor. Fabric wall pockets set at the appropriate height are useful for storing the most frequently used changing equipment while keeping the room clutter-free. (See page 80 for full instructions on how to make these.) Or fix castors to an old lidded box and store the nappy paraphernalia in it as a mobile changing unit.

A cupboard or wardrobe with doors will contain clothes that are still too big or already outgrown. Freestanding wardrobes or children's-size clothes rails are more versatile than a built-in system, unless it is tailor-made for children and designed to be upgraded at a later date.

An easy chair for comfortable feeding is also a must. A low, fairly upright, armless chair is usually recommended, though you may prefer one that has arms, so you can rest your elbows while feeding. If it is an old chair from another part of the house, cover it with a throw that works with the other colours in the room. A side table with a small light is also useful for resting books and a baby's drinks on.

It is a good idea to provide some sort of miniature seating. In the early days it can be used for displaying the soft toys new babies are inevitably showered with. Seating can take the form of small wicker chairs, sofas with lift-up seats, little rush-seated wooden chairs, tiny upholstered pieces or small wooden stools.

Baskets in vibrant colours that blend in with your scheme are ideal for babies' rooms. Buy several in a variety of sizes, and use them for laundry or toys or simply for decoration. Between the ages of 12 and 18 months, babies adore emptying and filling baskets with all manner of objects, so keep a small basket of toys in the kitchen, bathroom and living room, or any other room your child regularly follows you into.

It is never too early to invest in an old blanket box or a toy trunk for storing bits and pieces. It will be used for many years to come, for everything from toys and sports equipment to spare bedding and, if it has a lock, a teenager's secret letters and keepsakes.

Slumbering teddies prove that comfortable cushions and a soft yellow gingham fabric, pretty ducks and daffodils printed on furnishing cotton, deep frills and fringed trimmings do much to induce relaxation.

THE NURSERY:
FURNISHING SUGGESTIONS

Moses basket, crib or carrycot

Cot and mattress

Cot bumper

Crib sheets and cot sheets

Cellular crib and cot blankets

Cot quilt (do not use a pillow during a baby's first year)

Baby alarm

Baby bath or bath insert

Changing mat

Chest of drawers

Comfortable chair

Small side table and light

Storage for toys or bedlinen

Mobiles

Small chairs or stools

DETAILS

In many ways, the busier-looking a nursery, the better. Babies love colour and movement, so fix a musical mobile onto the cot, or above it, and a couple of other mobiles nearby. Site one near a doorway or window so any slight breeze or ray of light will cause it to twinkle and shimmer. Make your own mobiles from simple felt shapes, dismantled and painted egg cartons adorned with metallic paper flags, or tiny bells attached to wooden balls pierced with fine florists' wire. Always make sure that mobiles are fixed securely and there is no danger of their falling or being pulled into the crib or cot, or of bits coming off that the baby could swallow.

Try to think of the nursery from a baby's viewpoint. A pleasing tableau is of little use if it is too high up on a wall. It may look good to an adult walking into the room, but the baby will not be able to see it at all.

Peg rails or metal coat hooks are versatile additions to a nursery, allowing you to store and display clothes at the same time. Wax, stain or paint individual rails and arrange them in a continuous line or in twos or threes around the room. Use coathangers that blend with your theme – these could be padded hangers decorated with a delicate lace border, or painted wooden shapes such as clowns' heads.

For the walls, buy sheets of charming children's wrapping paper or colourful wallpapers or borders featuring the alphabet, numbers or animal illustrations and place them in simple clip frames. Change or rearrange them regularly to provide variety.

Make a display feature of heirloom china, porcelain dolls or battered well-loved old teddy bears in an antique glass-fronted display case mounted on the wall. Or create a faux dresser by fixing an old shallow bookcase against the wall to rest on top of a small chest of drawers. Strip or paint both pieces the same and display rag dolls, teddies and wooden toys on them.

THE DUCKS NURSERY

Animals are ideal starting points for decorating a nursery. The duck theme of our nursery (shown on pages 32–3) is neither too masculine nor too feminine, often an advantage if you want to decorate in advance of a new arrival. For the same reason, the yellow used on the walls and curtains is a sensible colour to choose. It is also extremely versatile, working equally well in small, dark rooms or in large, light rooms.

The duck theme emerged from the colourful wallpaper border that runs around the room at dado height. This particular border was chosen not only because ducks are so popular with children but also because it would quite happily make the transition from nursery to pre-school child's room. Like the theme itself, the colours of the border – a combination of green, blue and yellow – are suitable for boys or girls.

Repeating a motif from your fabric or furnishings as a decorative device on doors, covered boxes, walls or furniture is a good way to unify a scheme. You can make it as subtle or as obvious as your taste dictates. Here, we cut out the animal motifs from a length of coordinating fabric and used them repeatedly on a patchwork cot quilt.

The duck motifs are also used on both sides of the cupboard doors in the nursery. To keep the design simple, they are outlined in a heavy pencil line then coloured-in with watered-down paint for a pale, muted effect. On the back wall of the cupboard they are echoed with solid-yellow ducks applied with a stencil.

To transfer a drawing to a surface such as a stencil or cupboard door, first trace your motif from the wallpaper or border frieze onto tracing paper (or enlarge/reduce an image on a photocopier or using graph paper). Transfer it to the stencil card or to the cupboard door using carbon paper or by drawing the image on the reverse side of the tracing paper with a very soft pencil then laying the pencilled side against the surface and drawing or rubbing over the outlines from the front of the paper.

The duck motif used in the nursery is here repeated inside a cupboard. On the inside of the door, the ducks are painted freehand, while they are stencilled onto the wall at the back.

PATCHWORK COT QUILT OR PLAY MAT

As long as a quilt, bumper or, later on, duvet cover is made from pure, crisp cotton, it will serve as both a source of comfort and an inspiration to you and your child. Properly made, it will also become a treasured family heirloom to pass on to future generations. A quilt is at once useful, decorative and lasting – a treasured possession.

Quilts have a long and fascinating history, varying widely in design. Although many beautiful quilts are produced using only a single piece of fabric on top, it is patchwork that is most closely associated with quilting. Originally a thrifty method employed by country peasants as a means of keeping warm in the winter, it has become virtually an art form in itself.

These days, machine quilts can be just as pleasing as labour-intensive handmade quilts, and offer a time-saving way of creating something special for the nursery. With the addition of appliqué motifs or images, these quilts are frequently decorative enough to hang on the wall.

This cot quilt – which can also double as a play mat – incorporates fabric that coordinates with the wallpaper border, plus simple checks and stripes in colours that echo the walls and curtains, creating an effect which is coordinated, but not overly so. Using two checked, one striped and one patterned fabric, as here, you can make an endless variety of patterns from patchwork squares.

MEASURING

These instructions are for a quilt measuring 117 x 76cm (46 x 30in). It is made up of 15 blocks, each 20cm (8in) square, arranged in five rows of three blocks each, surrounded by a 10cm (4in) border. The unquilted dimensions are 122 x 81cm (48 x 32in); the quilting, however, makes it "shrink" a little. For the quilt to fit your cot exactly, it may be necessary to adjust the size of the blocks or border, or to alter the number of blocks.

YOU WILL NEED

FABRIC: SMALL CHECK, LARGE CHECK, STRIPE, DUCK PRINT AND PLAIN
MATCHING SEWING THREAD
MEDIUM-WEIGHT WADDING

1 From the duck fabric, cut out eight 22.5cm (9in) squares of fabric on the straight grain, each bearing a duck motif. From the small check, cut out one 22.5cm (9in) square on the diagonal and ten 12.5cm (5in) squares on the straight grain. From the striped fabric, cut out eight 12.5cm (5in) squares, four of them on the straight grain and four on the diagonal. Also from this fabric cut out eight 7.5 x 22.5cm (3 x 9in) rectangles.

2 With right sides together and raw edges even, join a checked square to a striped square, taking a 1.25cm (½in) seam. Repeat, then join the two pairs of squares to make one block. Make three more blocks of checked and striped squares in the same way. Press.

3 Again with right sides together and raw edges even, join a striped rectangle to one side of a checked square, taking a 1.25cm (½in) seam, starting and stopping 1.25cm (½in) in from each end. Stitch striped rectangles to the other three edges in the same way. Press. Mitre each corner by stitching with right sides together from the end of the stitching to the outside edge on the diagonal, as shown. Press.

4 Arrange the patches as shown in the photograph and stitch them together into rows, right sides together and taking 1.25cm (½in) seams. Press. Now stitch the rows together, taking care to match the seams.

5 From the small check, cut out four 7.5cm (3in) wide strips on the straight grain. Two of the strips should be the width of the patchwork portion, and the other two should be the length of the patchwork portion plus 12.5cm (5in). With right sides together and taking a 1.25cm (½in) seam, stitch a short strip to each end of the patchwork. In the same way, stitch a long strip to each side, so that the ends of the long strips are flush with the edges of the short strips. Press.

6 From the plain fabric, cut out four 6.5cm (2½in) wide strips on the straight grain. Two of the strips should be as long as the width of the quilt including the checked border, and two should be as long as the length of the quilt including the checked border. Fold one short strip in half lengthwise, wrong sides together, and lay it on top of the checked border at one end, with raw edges even. Stitch through all three thicknesses, taking a 1.25cm (½in) seam, and starting and stopping 1.25cm (½in) from the ends.

7 Fold the other strips in half lengthwise in the same way. Stitch the remaining short strip to the other end, and stitch the two long strips to the sides, again starting and stopping 1.25cm (½in) from the ends. Mitre the corners as in step 3. Press. For now, leave the plain border facing inwards, with the raw edges on the outside.

8 From the large-check fabric, cut a 135 x 94cm (53 x 37in) rectangle on the straight grain. From the wadding cut a 122 x 81cm (48 x 32in) rectangle.

9 Lay the large-check rectangle wrong side up on a flat surface and centre the wadding on top of it. Lay the patchwork right side up, centred on top of the wadding. Tack the quilt together through all layers around the outer edges and alongside the seams between blocks starting at the centre of the quilt and working outwards so that the fabric will be flat and smooth. Quilt by machine-stitching around the

edges of the blocks through all layers. Remove the tacking.

10 Turn under and press 1.25cm (½in) along the raw edges of the backing fabric and bring it over to the front, so the folded edge is even with the outer seamline. Stitch all around, along the edge. To mitre each corner, turn in the corner and trim off the point before folding the straight edges forward.

11 Turn the green border to the outside so it overlaps the large-check border, and topstitch along the inner edge through all layers.

DUCKS AND FLOWERS WALL HANGING

YOU WILL NEED
FABRIC: PLAIN AND CHECK
MATCHING SEWING THREAD
FELT: WHITE, ORANGE, TWO SHADES OF
YELLOW, BLACK
PVA ADHESIVE
NARROW DOWEL

The bold, naive style of fabric wall hangings makes them ideal for the nursery, particularly when they are large and colourful. This simple one has been designed to blend in with the nursery duck theme, but any simple motifs can be used. Position the hanging so your baby is able to see it from the cot, and move it around the room from time to time to provide variety. See the Templates at the back of the book for a selection of duck templates.

1 Cut out a rectangle of plain fabric to the desired size, adding 1.25cm (½in) all around for seam allowances. For the border cut two strips of checked fabric, on the straight grain, to the desired width – say, 10cm (4in) – plus 2.5cm (1in) for seam allowances, by the depth of the plain rectangle. Cut two more strips to the same width, by the width of the picture plus twice the width of the strip itself.

2 With right sides together and raw edges even, stitch the two shorter strips to the sides of the plain rectangle, taking a 1.25cm (½in) seam. Turn the borders to the right side and press. Stitch the other two strips to the top and bottom in the same way, with the ends flush with the side edges of the shorter strips. Turn to the right side and press.

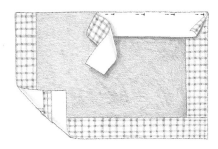

3 For the hanging loops, cut a 40.5 x 5cm (16 x 2in) length of checked fabric on the straight grain. Fold the long edges so they meet in the centre, then fold in half lengthwise; press and stitch. Cut into four equal lengths. Fold each one in half crosswise and place along the top edge of the hanging, on the right side. Position them so that the raw ends are at the top edge, and so that they are spaced equally across the hanging. Tack the loops in place.

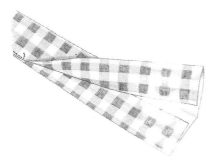

4 Cut a backing piece from the checked fabric, making it the same size as the front of the hanging. Position it on top of the other piece, right sides together. Stitch all around the edges

taking a 1.25cm (½in) seam and leaving a 15cm (6in) opening at the top of the seam on one side of the hanging. Trim the corners, turn right side out and press. Insert the dowel through the opening and hand sew it in place inside the wall hanging at the top.

5 Using the templates at the back of the book, and reducing/enlarging them as necessary, cut out the duck shapes from felt. Use white felt for the body and wing, orange for the feet and beak, and black for the eye of each duck. Glue these to the wall hanging using the photograph as a guide.

6 For each daffodil, cut out the six-petalled flower from felt in the lighter yellow and the circular centre from the slightly deeper yellow. Cut out small

Vs all around the edge of the centre. Glue in place.

7 For each daisy, cut a white circle, snip it irregularly around the edge and fan it out to make the shape slightly concave before sticking the centre to the fabric. Cut out a small orange circle and glue it in the middle of the white circle. Suspend the hanging from four small nails using the loops.

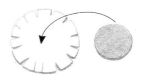

BUTTON-TRIMMED PELMET

This elegant pelmet, incorporating classic pinch pleats decorated with fabric-covered buttons, is a stylish solution for a nursery. Simple curtains can be made to appear much more special with the addition of a toning pelmet and tiebacks. Here, the plain fabric pelmet, which is accompanied by matching tiebacks, continues the yellow colour theme of the nursery. The tiebacks and the pinch pleats of the pelmet are decorated with buttons covered in the blue gingham used for the border of the wall hanging and for the Moses basket edging and quilt.

MOSES BASKET LINING AND QUILT

For the first two or three months of life, babies love the comfort and security provided by a snugly padded Moses basket. Lightly covered but protected by the high fabric-decorated sides of a soft carrying basket, they will sleep all the better. This basket has padded sides and a simple matching quilt.

Making the lining pattern

To ensure a perfect fit for your own basket, you will need to make a paper pattern from brown paper or newspaper. First make a pattern for the base. Inside the basket, cover the base with paper and run your fingers or scissors handles around the sides, then trim to shape. Label the top and bottom ends. Put this in place while you make the pattern for the sides.

Baskets are rarely symmetrical, so you'll need to make a pattern to go all the way around. Cut a rectangle to fit roughly around the top half and another for the bottom half, so they meet in the middle. Cut about six slits at regular intervals in each rectangle from the top almost to the bottom, so that each slit opens up to help the paper fit around the curving sides. Fill in the triangular space in each split with paper, sticking it in place with cellophane tape. Trim the top edge to 1.25cm (½in) below the top of the basket. You will now have two pieces shaped rather like fat boomerangs. Label which is the top half and which the bottom half.

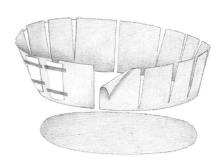

Basket lining

1 Use your base pattern to cut out one piece of main fabric for the base, adding 1.25cm (½in) all around for seam allowances. Fold the fabric in half and use each side pattern to cut two pieces of fabric on the bias, adding 2.5cm (1in) all around for seam allowances and for a "shrinkage" allowance caused by the quilting. For the edging, cut a 22.5cm (8½in) wide strip of contrasting fabric on the bias, making it long enough to fit all around the top plus 2.5cm (1in) for seams. Cut one piece of wadding for each half of the sides, the same size as the fabric pieces, and cut a 10cm (4in) wide strip of wadding the same length as the fabric piece for the edging.

2 Sandwich one piece of wadding between the two corresponding fabric pieces, right sides on the outside, and tack together all over by hand. Quilt by machine-stitching lines about 7cm (2¾in) apart in a grid pattern, using the check pattern as guide lines. Repeat for the other side piece.

3 With right sides together and raw edges even, stitch the two padded pieces together at both ends to form a ring, taking 1.25cm (½in) seams. Trim away the wadding within the seam allowances. Check that the padded ring fits inside the basket exactly, and adjust if necessary.

4 With right sides together and raw edges even, join the lower edges of the ring to the base, taking a 1.2cm (½in) seam. Trim away the wadding within the seam allowance, and clip the curves. Check again that it fits.

5 Tack the long strip of wadding to the wrong side of the strip of contrasting fabric along one long side, so the raw edges are even on that side. With right sides together and raw edges even, stitch the padded fabric strip around the top edge of the lining, taking a 1.25cm (½in) seam. Trim away the wadding within the seam allowance. Wrap the other half of the strip over the wadding, turn under 1.25cm (½in) and slipstitch to the outside.

6 Make six machine buttonholes near the folded edge of this padded strip, positioning one in the centre of each side and spacing the others equally. Cover the button forms with the main fabric, following the manufacturer's instructions, and sew these to the outside of the basket in line with the buttonholes. Insert the lining in the basket, and button in place.

Quilt

1 Cut out two rectangular pieces from the contrasting fabric, each measuring the width of the basket plus 20.5cm (8in) by the length of the basket plus 5cm (2in). Cut off the bottom corners in a continuous curve to fit the basket. Cut one piece of wadding to this size.

2 Sandwich the wadding between the two layers of fabric, and tack together all over. Machine quilt on a 12.5cm (5in) diagonal grid. Remove tacking.

3 Cut 8cm (3in) wide strips of the same fabric on the bias. Join the ends of the strips together to make enough bias binding to go around the quilt (see page 89, step 4). Turn under and press 6mm (¼in) along both raw edges, then fold the strip in half lengthwise, wrong sides together. Wrap the binding over the raw edges of the quilt to enclose them. Pin and then tack in place all around. Stitch through all layers; remove tacking.

CHAPTER FOUR

The Pre-School Years

The watershed between infancy and the pre-school years seems to occur at around the time when children need their first proper bed. From now on, their individual personalities emerge as specific likes and dislikes develop. Once the cot has been banished to the loft, or back to the nursery for child number two, the bedroom comes into its own, as the pre-school child emerges, assertive and irrepressibly inventive.

Whereas many children once lived close enough to open green spaces, where they could safely frolic in meadows and romp in woods, creating dens, treasure islands and imaginary worlds, their lives are often shaped today by a need to be supervised for their own safety, and by the dominant presence of the television, video recorder and computer. The end of the 20th century has brought with it a yearning for a return to simple values and to childhoods filled with simple magic once again.

During the last few decades children have been encouraged to become instant adults, missing out on some of the joys of innocent play, but you can recapture the fun of childhood by making their rooms stimulating and inviting – a good starting point for fun and learning, health and happiness.

A vibrant room packed with toys and activities is ideal for the pre-school child. In this Owl and the Pussycat Bedroom (see page 52), even the playhouse is decorated in colours that tone with the room.

ADAPTATIONS

Turning a nursery into a pre-school bedroom may be simply a matter of changing a cot for a bed, buying a wardrobe and acquiring a small desk and chair. However, it is rarely so straightforward. As your baby becomes a small person, you will probably find yourself redecorating or deciding how to make the most of the available space in the room. Yet if you have planned the nursery with all these adaptations at the back of your mind, the transition should be relatively easy and, above all, fun.

Children of this age often share the same room, either owing to lack of space in the home or out of preference. For this arrangement to work well, try to reflect both personalities in your scheme. If one is a bookworm and the other an actor, make sure there is provision for plenty of bookshelves and a dressing-up corner. Try to provide varied storage, and give some thought to the beds. Two single beds that can be adapted to form bunks later on could be a good temporary solution.

DECORATING

The ages of two to five are the years in which your furnishings will get some of the heaviest wear and tear in terms of spills and rough treatment, so it's best to think ahead and plan your use of fabrics and wallpapers accordingly. A good way of allowing for the odd replacement of wallpaper or mop-up operation is to choose a kind of wallcovering that divides the wall in some way. For example, a wallpaper border at chair rail height, with washable emulsion paint below, and striped, spotty or floral wallpaper above, will prove a versatile solution for the "messy" years.

On the windows, it is a good idea to have some form of blackout lining to prevent early

The sky at night in naive form is depicted in this simple stencilled frieze, transforming a part of the room that is often left plain white. A colourwash wallpaper provides the stripes. The design will appeal to any age group.

morning awakenings in the summer months. A combination of a roller or Roman blind, backed with blackout lining, together with a pair of simple, lightweight curtains, is a good solution. Team them with a simple pelmet, scalloped for a feminine feel or zigzagged for boys, and you will have a complete window treatment that is both visually appealing and practical.

Young children adore colour, so window treatments offer a good chance of combining contrasting colours or fabrics. Team spots with stripes, flowers with plain fabrics and bold checks with small checks. Allow your children to decide on a theme themselves and help decide where they appear – if you want to limit their impact, suggest a duvet cover emblazoned with the favourite animal or person and echo the colours in the room.

BEDS AND BEDLINEN

The bed is the one piece of equipment that merits special thought, as it will probably last your child into the teenage years. Now is the time to consider a bunk bed if you have other children or are thinking of expanding the family, although children should not sleep on a top bunk before they are six years old. A platform bed or cabin bed with a desk and den space underneath may be the answer for a small room, or a box bed with baskets underneath in a traditional interior. Make sure that the mattress is firm and that the bed is the right size. Some antique beds are quite short and narrow so would not last very long for a tall child.

You can, to some extent, dictate the feel of a bedroom by your choice of bedlinen. If you have bold coloured walls emblazoned with strong, simple motifs, then the chances are you will need an equally vibrant duvet cover or bedspread. If you cannot find a ready-made duvet cover of your choice, make your own. It's a simple operation to choose fabric that goes with your scheme, give it a turn-over in a contrasting colour trimmed with buttons, ties or bows and make a pillowcase to match – as we did for our Owl and the Pussycat Bedroom.

Contrasting fabric was used to trim this duvet cover with a buttoned turn-over, while the pillowcase was given a similar treatment. Details like these look just as smart in a pre-school child's bedroom as in an older child's or adult's room.

A PLAY PALACE

Children of pre-school age are highly social, thriving on the company of their contemporaries and relishing the thought of busy days, full of creative pursuits and a rich fantasy life. To provide the ideal environment for children to immerse themselves in another world it is worth putting some effort into making their rooms as interesting and magnetic as possible.

Play is an important part of the learning process for young children. Dressing-up games involving real or make-believe characters, games featuring the buying and selling of myriad items in pretend stores and games involving miniature worlds of play people, soft toys, pirates or soldiers, all help develop the imagination and emotions of a young child.

Another opportunity for your child to learn is through play-acting with plenty of props and equipment. A dressing-up box (maybe the blanket box you had in the nursery) is a favourite possession of many children and is often fondly remembered in later life. In fact, dressing-up boxes are essential equipment in young children's rooms. Their urge to step out of themselves and become any of a host of storybook characters, from fairies to pirates, is very strong. A block-printed, stencilled, hand-painted or découpaged chest or box in the corner of a room will not only contain all the paraphernalia but will also provide inspiring decoration in its own right. The box in our Owl and the Pussycat Bedroom was simply colour-washed and then potato-printed with stars.

Simple treasure in the form of highly decorative dressing-up clothes will be donned much more often if stored in a magical painted box. This one was decoratd with stars in accordance with our Owl and the Pussycat theme.

DISPLAYING TOYS

At this age, pigeon-hole shelves come into their own, either as a freestanding unit or built into an alcove or across an entire wall of the room. Use them for displaying distinct types of toys such as skittles, wooden animals, toy musical instruments, miniature tea-sets, cars or books.

Fill old printers' trays with antique wooden building blocks, dolls' house accessories, tiny Noah's Ark animals, brooches and badges. Change the displays every so often and hide some things away from time to time in a cupboard or wardrobe – rediscovering toys is exciting, especially on wet winter days.

Miniature worlds in the form of dolls' houses, play houses, forts and farms are popular toys at this stage, particularly when they have been made by parents or relatives. Make sure there is enough floor or table space for your child to spread out all the small accessories, such as people, animals, kitchen equipment, furniture and scraps of fabric. They are the vital props that will bring these tiny scenes to life.

CREATING MORE STORAGE

When a nursery becomes more of a bedroom, you will inevitably need to find extra storage space. If the bed you have chosen has space underneath it, capitalize on it by adding drawers, baskets or crates on castors. Stacking boxes or baskets are space-saving containers for building blocks and other small items. They will fit happily underneath a bottom shelf or at the foot of a wardrobe. In an under-used alcove, consider fitting a chrome clothes rail at a height where your child can reach their own clothes. It will encourage them to dress themselves and exercise choice in what they wish to wear. (Make sure you display only the clothing you would like them to wear, though!) You can cover the clothes rail with a simple fabric blind. Insert eyelets along the top edge of the blind, lace cord through the holes and lash it to a shelf fitted into the alcove above the rail.

Freestanding toy cupboards – securely fixed to the wall if there is any chance they could be pulled over – are versatile pieces of furniture. They can be painted to echo your decorative theme, or left plain and embellished with panels of fabric or wooden fretwork. To keep small toys away from babies in the house, consider mounting open-topped wooden boxes onto the wall and painting the fronts with blackboard paint so they double as wall-mounted easels and toy boxes. At this age, children start to take an interest in height charts. Mount one on the wall near a doorway.

FLOORS AND WALLS

If you had a painted floor in the nursery, then there is no need to change it for this stage of childhood. Youngsters in this phase do everything at speed, so non-slip and wipeable flooring is a distinct advantage now. Cork tiles provide a neutral-coloured, practical surface, while carpet tiles are individually replaceable should spills and stains spoil it in places. If nursery motifs have become too babyish, try painting the floor a totally different colour to provide some variety.

Walls can become decorative elements in their own right. Children are delighted by big images which tell a story. If you feel inclined, have a go at painting a scene from your child's favourite classic fairy tale or cartoon character. If you use muted colours, you can always paint over the wall when the mural has been outgrown.

Encourage your child's creative skills by pinning up their best efforts on a pinboard and framing any particular favourites. Or create a special area of the wall to use for their pictures (see page 110).

Devise a special frieze made up of your child's own images. Get them to draw a specific scene which bears repetition around the room – such as a vase of flowers, a simple house complete with spotty curtains, or stick figures – then photocopy the image, enlarging it if necessary. Ask your child to colour in each one, then mount them together on the wall at dado height, using PVA glue. These borders are infinitely replaceable and children will love being able to create their own friezes for their rooms.

THE PRE-SCHOOL BEDROOM:
SUGGESTED FURNISHINGS

Bed with underbed storage, or bunk or platform bed

Small table and two chairs for creative activities

Painting easel

Height chart

Pinboard for photographs, paintings and drawings

Additional storage shelves or bookcase

Dressing-up box

THE OWL AND THE PUSSYCAT BEDROOM

Our Owl and the Pussycat Bedroom (shown on pages 46–7) was designed around the needs and interests of children aged two to five. They adore having a galaxy of activities strewn around their rooms: nooks and crannies offering inviting space for playhouses and dressing-up clothes; small chairs and a table for mock tea parties; baskets laden with books; vibrant colours and their own artwork adorning the walls all make the room as appealing as possible.

This particular scheme is suitable for a girl or boy. The Owl and Pussycat wallpaper border was the starting point, suggesting a star-and-moon theme in a blue and yellow colour scheme. Striped wallpaper is contrasted with bold checked fabric and chambray-blue woodwork. Elsewhere in the room a bold checked fabric is used for the curtains and cabina. The bedlinen fabric is a simple, painterly floral with a small check design in it that tones with the chambray blue and apple green of the big check. All these fabrics and wallpapers were chosen for their bold colours and also because they were designs a child would not grow out of. (See page 29 for how they can be adapted as the child gets older.)

CUT-OUT LAMPSHADE

Lampshades can be adapted to match the decorative theme of a child's room. Trace some simple shapes (here the motifs echo the moons and stars on the walls above the picture rail) around the shade using a pencil; then, with a sharp craft knife, carefully cut out the shapes. Alternatively, glue on small decorative pieces such as tiny shells, pieces of knotted rope or sequins and buttons.

FOUR-POSTER BED FRAME

Wooden four-poster surrounds for children's beds such as that shown here are fun to make but should only be tackled by someone with experience of carpentry. They can range from four simple posts draped with fabric to elaborate shapes formed with a jigsaw. Another idea is to attach shallow panels that echo the base of the bed frame then stick on wallpaper borders, cut-out shapes or three-dimensional images such as fabric animal motifs or wooden building blocks. Alternatively, paint on shapes freehand, or use stencils or sponging for a slightly different effect. See the Templates section at the back of the book for ideas.

This bed frame simply fits over an existing divan bed. The easiest way to construct it is by building it *in situ*. Use 5 x 5cm (2 x 2in) posts at the corners; ours are 2m (79in) high, but the exact height will depend on the height of your ceiling. Be sure to allow adequate clearance above the bed. When planning the horizontal dimensions of the framework, allow a little room between the frame and the mattress for bedding.

The posts are joined with eight 30cm- (12in-) deep lengths of 1.25cm- (½in-) thick MDF; use four at the bottom (at divan height) and four at the top as a pelmet. Cut star shapes out of the pelmet strips at regular intervals using a drill and a jigsaw, then attach all eight lengths of MDF with countersunk screws. Paint the whole framework, and decorate the base with a wallpaper border.

PLAYHOUSE

This easy-to-construct playhouse has three hinged walls and a removable roof. It could be further simplified by making it in hardboard and dispensing with the roof. If it can be sited in a corner, it can have just two walls, making it more portable. Children will love going in and out the door, so add to their fun with a letter box and a bicycle bell for a doorbell.

MEASURING

Decide how big a playhouse you would like and cut out three pieces of MDF accordingly. (You do not need a fourth piece because the open side of the house will be against a wall.) If you wish the walls to fold flat for storage, the two side walls will have to be no more than half the width of the middle wall.

1 Taking the piece of MDF for the front of the house first, cut out the main window with a jigsaw. Use water-based paint to transform it into a house or a shop. Remember to paint both sides, as one will be inside the house. Next, cut four 5cm (2in) strips of MDF to fit around the window. Paint these a different colour from the walls if you wish. Screw in place. Small pieces can be glued instead.

2 Cut out a window and door opening and repeat the process for the door wall, but use a 7.5cm (3in) strip of MDF for the bottom horizontal piece of the door frame. Paint. Repeat again for the third wall.

3 The simplest method of joining the three panels together is to fix two long metal hinges to the inside edges where each panel joins the next, so the walls can be folded lat. Covering the hinged edge with strong, thick, black tape will add strength and prevent children from scratching themselves, but will prevent it from folding up. Similarly, vertical supports can be added on the inside at the corners for extra strength, but these too will prevent the play-house from folding flat.

4 For the door, cut a piece of MDF to fit the opening. Cut a hole in it for the letterbox, then cut a piece of MDF for the flap. Attach this over the opening with hinges, covering the hinged edge with the tape.

5 Finally, attach the door to the door frame with hinges, and paint the whole surface.

6 To make the serving hatch shelf, cut a piece of MDF 10cm (4in) wide, and as long as you want the shelf to be. Paint it, then leave to dry. Attach it to the window frame with strong, thick tape. Allow the shelf to fold down when not in use. To hold it up when it is being used, fix cup hooks to the upper surface of the shelf and attach

1.25CM (½IN) THICK MDF
METAL HINGES
STRONG, THICK BLACK TAPE
WOODEN DOWELLING
JIGSAW
METAL CHAIN, CUP HOOKS AND SCREW EYES
NAILS AND SCREWS
WOODEN DOOR KNOB
WOOD GLUE
WATER-BASED PAINTS
BICYCLE BELL

chains to the inside edge of the window frame.

7 Make and attach the serving hatch door in the same way but attach the hooks to its bottom outside edge and the screw eyes to the roof.

8 Made from four pieces of MDF, the roof is hinged down the middle and on both sloping edges of each end. For strength you ccould cover the hinged edges with the black tape. Dowels can also be used to give the roof additional rigidity. Drill two holes (shaped like elongated circles to allow for the slope) on the front and two more, in line with the first two, on the back, then insert the dowels. Finally, paint the whole surface.

CABINA

Fabric-covered wardrobes like this delightful checked cabina are wonderfully versatile storage solutions for children's rooms. Choose a wooden frame of shelves, or shelves plus a hanging rail, to cover with the fabric. As your child grows, you can either remove the fabric to reveal a simple set of storage shelves or change the fabric cover to suit the child's new tastes.

YOU WILL NEED

WOOD FRAME

FABRIC

MATCHING SEWING THREAD

MEASURING

This cabina is 185cm (73in) high, 120cm (47in) wide and 91cm (36in) deep, but you can adjust the measurements as much as you wish.

For the back, cut a panel of fabric the width of the back plus 4cm (1½in), by the height of the back plus 6.5cm (2½in). For the sides, cut two panels each the width of the side plus 4cm (1½in), by the height of the side plus 6.5cm (2½in). For the front, cut two panels each half the width of the front plus 6cm (2¼in), by the height of the front plus 6.5cm (2½in). Remember when cutting the panels to ensure the pattern matches all the way around.

A 4cm (1½in) hem is included in the above measurements, but if you prefer a deeper one – ours is 13cm (5in) or so – add extra to each panel. If you are using very wide fabric or making a cover for a small cabina, you may be able to cut the front and side panels as one piece, or possibly even use just two panels, which meet at centre back.

For the top, cut a panel the width of the frame plus 4cm (1½in), by the depth of the frame plus 4cm (1½in).

For the zigzag edge, cut 23cm (9in) wide strips on the bias. Join to form two strips as long as the width of the frame plus twice the depth of the frame plus 15cm (6in), being careful to match the pattern.

For the four ties, cut four 40.5 x 5cm (16 x 2in) strips on the straight grain.

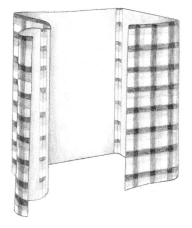

1 With right sides together and raw edges even, stitch each front panel to a side panel, taking a 2cm (¾in) seam and matching the pattern at the seamline. Stitch the side panels to the back panel in the same way.

2 Turn under 1.25cm (½in) and then 4cm (1½in) on the centre front edge and on the lower edge all around. Press and stitch.

3 To make the ties, fold the long raw edges of each strip to meet in the centre, then fold in half lengthwise. Press and stitch, turning under the raw edges at each end. Hand sew the ties to the wrong side on both front opening edges, positioning one pair about a quarter of the way down and the other pair about halfway down.

4 For the zigzag edging, place the fabric strip with right sides together and raw edges even. Make a zigzag template with the triangles each 12.5cm (5in) high. Place it 7.5cm (3in) from the fold and 1.25cm (½in) from each end; draw around the template. Stitch along the marked lines. Trim the fabric 6mm (¼in) from the stitching, cutting off the outer corners and clipping into the inner corners within the seam allowance. Turn right side out and press. Turn in the raw edges at the ends, press and slipstitch.

5 On the right side, pin and tack the zigzag piece around the top, with the raw edges even.

6 Turn under and press 2cm (¾in) on all four edges of the top panel. With right sides together, pin, tack and stitch the joined front, side and back panels (and zigzag edging) to the top panel, matching the seams to the corners and stitching one side at a time so you can stop at the seamline in each corner. Clip into the corners within the seam allowance. Remove any remaining tacking that is visible, and then press.

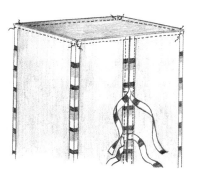

THE AMAZON BEDROOM

You can almost hear the Amazonian waterfalls and far-off screeching parakeets in this jungle-inspired room. Using the multi-coloured wallpaper border as a starting point, we drew on the wildlife motifs to create a tropical den. The bed, with its camouflage canopy, is the tent from which explorers venture forth after a cosy night's sleep. The hammock harbours teddies and dolls, keeping dry, and the rug, complete with menacing crocodile, is the place where you play at your peril. Fabrics are kept plain and simple as befits a rugged tropical outpost, but colours are vivid jungle tones of blue-green, red and orange.

At this age, children will love to join in decision-making and helping with simple tasks. Many of the smaller projects involve cutting out and gluing, which are ideal for small children. They will delight in attaching their finished creations to the walls and other surfaces.

Dripping with jungle imagery, our Amazon Bedroom is more an adventure playground than a bedroom. Translucent tropical-green walls seem to extend all over the room, with toning shades on toy boxes and bed curtains, while animals are everywhere, apparently leaping out from the wallpaper border to adorn rugs, curtains and the bed. Tie-top curtains with boldly coloured borders and appliquéd parakeets serve the dual purpose of blocking out the light and adding to the jungle scene.

GIRAFFE EASEL

Customize a painting easel to match the mood of the day or the room theme. Children will love to make their own decisions about this. Encourage them to paint whole pictures or patterns.

JUNGLE BOX

Painted in two shades of rain forest green, this chest can be used for jungle clothes and pith helmet – or simply as a place to keep clutter. Decorate it with animal stickers or cut-out images from the wallpaper border to echo the other animals in the room. You could also photocopy the images so your child can colour them in. Alternatively, paint on palm trees and banana leaves or bamboo and bulrushes. After painting the box and gluing the images on, apply several coats of varnish, allowing it to dry between coats.

CHANGING JUNGLE SCENE

To complete the jungle fever theme, create a movable felt picture, in which children can move the constituent parts around to create their own jungle scenes. Cover a standard cork noticeboard with deep green felt, attaching the felt at the back with a staple gun or fabric glue.

Next, attach vertical strips of self-adhesive Velcro. These represent the trunks of palm trees. Cut out palm fronds and jungle animals from felt, and stick Velcro on the back of each. Children can then arrange and rearrange the animals against the background of palm trees.

COLOURWASHED WALLS

The atmospheric green walls of our Amazon Bedroom were created by applying a pale yellow basecoat to the wall. When it was dry, a coat of blue-green water-based paint, diluted to a thin wash, was lightly applied on top to create a vivid but translucent texture, evoking a tropical rain forest. You can also buy wallpapers that imitate this paint effect.

BUNKBED COVER

YOU WILL NEED

MAIN FABRIC

MATCHING SEWING THREAD

PRESS STUDS

LARGE EYELETS AND EYELET TOOL

THICK CORD

SEW-AND-STICK VELCRO

ACRYLIC PAINTS OR FABRIC PAINTS

This tent-like bunkbed cover is formed from three canvas panels, attached to the bed frame with Velcro. It transforms the bed into a jungle playhouse and even incorporates a roll-up window for intrepid explorers. The tropical vegetation has been applied with acrylic paint, but fabric paint is equally effective and is washable. Or decorate the tent using appliquéd, stencilled or sponged designs.

MEASURING

Measure the bunkbed to establish the size of the panels, and add 4.5cm (1¾ in) all around for hems.

1 Cut out three canvas panels. If your fabric isn't wide enough, join widths using flat felt seams. Hem all four edges of each panel by pressing under 5mm (¼in) and then 4cm (1½in); machine stitch, mitring the corners (see page 41, step 10).

2 On one side panel, create a window by cutting out a rectangle about the size of this book. Make a 5cm (2in) snip diagonally into each corner. Turn under the raw edges to make a double hem on each edge; stitch.

3 To make the window flap, cut out a canvas rectangle 13cm (5in) wider than the window opening and 14.5cm (5½in) deeper. Stitch a double 1.25cm (½in) hem on the side and bottom edges. For the two straps, cut two strips of fabric, each measuring 9 x 30.5cm (3½in x 12in). Fold each in half, right sides together, and stitch down the side and across one end,

taking a 5mm (¼in) seam. Turn the straps right side out.

4 To attach the window flap to the panel, position it above the window opening, right sides together, with the raw edge of the flap a little above the top of the window. Insert the two straps between the flap and the panel, with the raw edges even with those of the flap. Stitch across the flap, taking a 4cm (1½in) seam. Turn down the flap

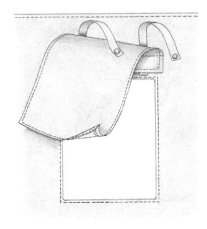

so it covers the window opening, with the straps hanging down on top. Attach press studs to the ends, with the other halves on the panel just above the window opening. Use the straps to hold the flap when rolled up.

5 On the other side panel, attach an eyelet at the bottom (at the edge that will be in the centre). Thread a length of cord through it, and use to tie the panel back onto the bed frame. You could also attach one to the side panel with the window if you want to.

6 Machine stitch the sew-on side of a strip of Velcro to the top edge of each panel and stick the self-adhesive side to the bed frame.

7 Decorate the panels by whichever method you choose. If you use fabric paints, fix them following the manufacturer's instructions so the panels will be hand-washable.

TIE-TOP JUNGLE CURTAINS

These cheery jungle curtains, replete with vividly coloured parakeets, will enliven any window view. Unlined for simplicity, they are finished off with bound edges and ties, and can match or contrast with your chosen motifs for the bunkbed cover. Either fabric or felt can be used for making the bird shapes but, if you use felt, you'll have to dry-clean the curtains rather than wash them.

YOU WILL NEED

MAIN CURTAIN FABRIC
CONTRASTING FABRIC
MATCHING SEWING THREAD
FELT OR FABRIC FOR APPLIQUÉ SHAPES
FUSIBLE WEB
STRANDED EMBROIDERY COTTON

MEASURING

For the curtain fabric, you will need a little less than 1½ times the width of the pole, since too much fullness would obscure the appliquéd birds. To calculate the length, measure from the pole to wherever you want the curtains to end, and add 15cm (6in).

1 Cut out the curtains from the main fabric, and join widths if necessary. From the contrasting fabric, cut 10cm (4in) wide strips on the straight grain. Join the ends until you have enough to bind all around the edges of the curtains. Fold the binding in half lengthwise, wrong sides together, and press. Now fold the raw edges in almost to the centre, and press.

2 Encase the raw edges of the curtain sides and bottom in the folded binding. Pin in place and topstitch. Mitre the corners at the bottom end by folding the binding diagonally. Finally, bind the top edge in the same way, turning in the raw ends at each side rather than mitring the corners.

3 The curtain ties are made from strips of a different colour but the same type of fabric. Cut out enough 45 x 5cm (18 x 2in) strips for your curtain width, allowing for them to be spaced about 20.5cm (8in) apart. Turn under 6mm (¼in) on each long side and press. Fold the strips in half lengthwise, wrong sides together, then press again. Stitch the folded sides together. Sew the strips securely to the back of the curtain, at the top.

4 Use the templates at the back of the book to cut out the parakeet shapes from fusible web. Iron the shapes onto pieces of felt, following the manufacturer's instructions, then cut out the shapes in felt. Peel off the backing paper and iron the felt shapes to the right side of the curtain. Embroider around the outer edges using a large slipstitch or a large cross-stitch and several strands of embroidery cotton.

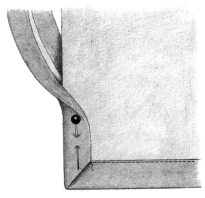

TEDDIES' HAMMOCK

This cotton hammock provides a restful, not to mention tidy, retreat for the dolls and soft toys. If you want it to hold a very large collection of soft toys, hang it in a corner, perhaps attached to the wall and a bed, as here, or to a peg rail fixed onto adjacent walls. Be sure to hang it where a child cannot try to climb into it.

YOU WILL NEED

THICK CANVAS OR
UPHOLSTERY-WEIGHT FABRIC
MATCHING SEWING THREAD
12 LARGE EYELETS AND EYELET TOOL
2 LARGE CURTAIN RINGS
WHITE CORD

1 Cut a 90 x 120cm (36 x 48in) piece of fabric. Fold in half crosswise with right sides together. Stitch a 1.25cm (½in) seam down the side, leaving an opening for turning right side out.

2 Refold so that the seam runs down the middle. Stitch across both ends taking a 1.25cm (½in) seam. Trim seams and clip corners. Turn right side out, slipstitch the opening and press.

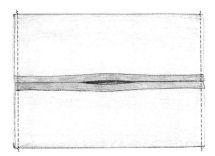

3 Using the eyelet tool, attach eyelets at 5cm (2in) intervals at both ends.

4 At each end, lace a length of cord back and forth through the eyelets and the curtain ring.

5 Hang the finished hammock on two fixed hooks or on one hook and the bed frame.

APPLIQUÉD SWAMP RUG

This decorated rug doubles as a playmat, instantly becoming a treacherous swamp whenever a child wishes. Use a bright, nubbly cotton rug as your backdrop and create a scene or still life on a water theme. If crocodiles are too frightening, then apply some waterlilies and a few leaping frogs, or a fishing fleet and a shoal of mackerel. A green rug could form a meadow for dragonflies, small birds and ripening wheat, or a bold swathe of sunflowers.

1 Using the templates at the back of the book, cut out the shapes, adding a 6mm (¼in) seam allowance all around to the fabric shapes. (Felt shapes do not need a seam allowance.) Cut the stepping stones from the biscuit-coloured linen or jute. Cut the main part of the crocodile from the lighter green fabric. Cut the crocodile's scaly back from the darker green fabric as follows: using the wide template, cut four pieces of which two are in reverse; using the short, narrow template, cut one piece; using the long, narrow template, cut two pieces of which one is in reverse. Cut the crocodile's features and the water-lilies from felt.

2 Turn under 6mm (¼in) all around the edges of the stepping stones and zigzag stitch. Stitch the flower centres to the flowers. Turn under a narrow hem all around the edges of the crocodile's body and head; stitch.

3 Stitch a long, narrow dart down the centre of the crocodile's head, on the right side. Stitch the crocodile's eyes to his head, gluing on the black felt pieces. For his nostrils, cut two crescent shapes from the green felt nose, and back the holes with black felt; stitch around the edge of each nostril then stitch the nose to the head.

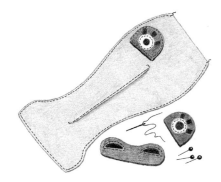

4 Join the segments of the crocodile, with right sides together, taking 6mm (¼in) seams.

5 For the wide part of the scaly back, pin one of the wide shapes to its mirror image, right sides together, and stitch along the straight edge taking a 6mm (¼in) seam. Repeat for the other two identical shapes. Now lay these two pieces with right sides together, and stitch all around the edges, taking a 6mm (¼in) seam and leaving an opening. Turn right side out, press and slipstitch the opening.

6 For the piece that goes on top, turn under 6mm (¼in) all around the short, narrow back piece and press. Centre it on top of the wide back piece and stitch around the edge of the top piece. Now hand sew the whole piece to the crocodile's body.

7 Pin the two long, narrow back pieces with right sides together. Stitch all around the edge, taking a 6mm (¼in) seam and leaving an opening in the straight side for turning. Turn right side out, press and stitch to the crocodile's tail along the straight edge.

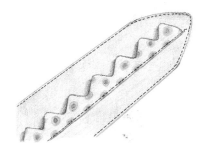

8 Position the crocodile diagonally across the rug, and the stepping stones so they meander across the other diagonal. Scatter the water-lilies over the remaining surface. Hand sew all the pieces in place around the edges.

CHAPTER FIVE

The Primary School Years

O nce children start school, their lives, and yours, change dramatically. Their independence, already established with small friends arriving for tea and play, is further extended, with after-school activities and weekend visits further afield. This is the age when boys and girls, who may have previously played happily together for hours on end, become polarized for a while – the boys not wishing to be associated with girls and their dolls, the girls disliking too much rough and tumble in the playground.

School also means a compulsion to be like everyone else, the necessity for possessing the latest toy craze and a need to collect all sorts of ephemera and natural booty, from lurid stickers to seaside flotsam and jetsam. All these extra possessions will need extra storage space, both small-scale and large-scale. Children of this age will certainly have an opinion about their rooms, with very specific colour preferences. Where possible, encourage them to partake in any redecoration or space-planning jobs. They may particularly enjoy applying motifs to walls, floor and fixtures or painting shapes onto calico for making up into small curtains.

A life on the ocean waves seems perfectly possible in this Sailor's Bedroom (see page 74). Armed with a boat bed that looks almost sea-worthy, real sails and lengths of bunting, adventurous children can immerse themselves in all sorts of imaginary nautical adventures. Jaunty stripes in the classic colour combination of red, white and blue adorn duffel bags, simple window blinds, bunting and cushions, while boat motifs appear on the duvet fabric and are appliquéd to crisp white pillowcases.

ROOM TO GROW

Older primary-school children tend to spend most of their time in their rooms, playing with friends, or at the kitchen table, seeking help with difficult homework. They are constantly on the go, creating wear, tear and torture on all sorts of indoor surfaces from floors and walls to fabric and furniture, so make sure that any new furniture you acquire at this stage will withstand disrespectful treatment in the form of swinging, climbing and performing youngsters.

At this stage of their lives, children appreciate as much space as possible to spread out train sets, farmyards, miniature car sets and complicated board games. Since accidental spills and messy play lessen, you could quite happily lay a durable carpet at this stage. Or, if you prefer wooden floorboards, you could think about investing in a more expensive rug, which will last until your child leaves home, and could then be pressed into service elsewhere.

An area of the room devoted to study is essential now. It should comprise a desk, a serviceable lamp and a sturdy chair, together with shelving for books, a waste bin and, ideally, an additional work/play surface. This comes in handy for homework that needs extra space and also as a place to keep small pets such as gerbils, hamsters, tadpoles or goldfish, not to mention miniature gardens of cress, broad beans or bulbs and nature collections such as shells and stones, twigs and leaves. Children of this age seem to accumulate treasures from a variety of sources, including school, friends and the great outdoors.

Don't discard any miniature tables and chairs your pre-school child may have used. They will still be very useful for playing-card and board games and for practising reading and writing.

Try to incorporate a small, freestanding mirror and brush and comb to encourage youngsters to smarten themselves up before leaving for school. Girls in particular enjoy having some kind of dressing table in which they can store their jewellery and knick-knacks. The easiest way to create one would be to cover a circular topped table in the fabric of her choice. The top of a chest of drawers gives ample opportunity for a miniature dressing table, complete with small wicker baskets containing scarves and hats. Boys may be more content with a basketful of catapults, water pistols and football cards.

DECORATING

At this age, children particularly like themed rooms. Our Sailor's Bedroom shown on pages 68–9 is many a young boy's dream. Inspired by the fabric used for the duvet, which has boats, planes and cars on it, it has been designed around a specially built bed. Everything else in the room could easily be adapted once the child has outgrown this particular passion. But, in the meantime, where better to fend off marauding pirates than from the comfort and safety of your own bed, complete with "secret" storage compartments in the stern for hidden treasure. At the other end of the room, a real dinghy – preferably a small one – piled with cushions could provide a reading area, as well as a wonderful setting for a game.

Other popular themes include knights and heraldic symbols, toy soldiers, circuses and football motifs for boys. A border of cut-out life-sized footballs would be a graphic way of dividing a wall, as would a series of heraldic shields or banners, coloured in different tones and styles. Appliqué similar shapes onto plain fabric or use a particular themed border as the starting point for a scheme.

For girls, try simple flower shapes, or floral fabrics, simple checks and stripes, or a polkadot den, with differing sizes of dots on bedlinen, window treatments and frills around a tabletop. Team with a pelmet embellished with bows, or make a simple tie blind with fabric rosettes ranged across it at regular intervals. To provide some contrast with accessories, cover boxes, line baskets or make drawstring bags in contrasting fabrics.

Box-seat cushions, bolsters and throws are another useful way of incorporating fabric in a room, providing a good counterpoint to the bedlinen and curtains.

The fabrics chosen for both our Little Princess's Bedroom (see page 83) and the Sailor's Bedroom are not particularly childish in style. However, they have been used in an imaginative way: four-poster-style bed hangings, or strings of flags flying above a bed, create the feeling that the bed is sailing on the high seas or set in a

Painted furniture is a successful way of enhancing the decoration in a room. Use matching or contrasting colours, add découpaged shapes or painted imagery – such as the painted portholes of this boat bed in our Sailor's Bedroom (page 74) – and protect the finished product with a coat of water-based varnish.

fairy-tale castle. At this stage of childhood, using adult fabrics can work very well. Fresh-looking checks, simple stripes and subtly patterned damask all work for both sexes and are durable as well as pleasing. They can be used in any number of ways, such as plain window blinds, window-seat covers, pleated bed valances, simple drapes that curtain off a bed or gently gathered curtains combined with a castellated or scalloped pelmet.

For open shelves, floors and beds, buy plain canvas and decorate it with colours, patterns or motifs that have been chosen by your child. (The waves on page 78 are delightfully simple to achieve.) Use the finished design as a blind, wall hanging, door curtain or rug.

Another good way to unify a scheme is to use fabric or wallpaper to cover rough-edged tea chests for toy storage. Or paint metal trunks and decorate them with découpaged shapes or motifs to blend in with the theme – whether pirates, cartoon characters or bunches of flowers.

If your child has definitely outgrown the design on their bedlinen, make a new duvet cover and pillowcase, or appliqué motifs onto plain calico using blanket stitch.

At this age, children are capable of helping you with painting or decorating jobs. Enlist their help in sanding and painting furniture, choosing fabric and deciding on motifs. They will enjoy looking in magazines and catalogues for inspiration. Let them tell you what they like before you unconsciously impose your preferences on them. Give them the confidence to express their likes and dislikes, even if their suggestions appall you – you can always accommodate their choices on detailing such as cupboard door panels, bedheads or wall friezes.

STORAGE

You will still need to store some pre-school toys in this older child's room, so they can be rediscovered from time to time. Older children take great nostalgic comfort from their early toys and enjoy renewed acquaintance with their younger years every so often.

Additional storage space is likely to be needed for new possessions such as games, chemistry sets, musical instruments, binoculars and flower presses. Either add on extra shelves to an existing system or think about a freestanding cupboard or chest of drawers for tidying away board games and sports equipment. A cabina (page 56) is as valuable now as in a younger child's room.

Extra storage can always be created in a modular bed system or by devoting one wall or alcove to fitted pigeon-holes. Vary their sizes so you can fit in anything from encyclopedias to cricket pads, rag dolls to footballs.

A bedside table is useful at this age, for an alarm clock, a light, some reading matter and a drink. It also encourages a child to develop some independence in the mornings and evenings.

Fabric wall pockets are useful for tidying away trainers and plimsolls, as well as dressing-up scarves, hats and shoes.

If you decide to buy a bed that is a modular unit of some kind, think about installing a shelving system within a canopied bed (see page 90) or underneath the mattress. Or, if space permits, place the bed away from one wall and put a chest of drawers up against it, to double as a bedhead and additional storage space.

HOMEWORK CORNER

Children will spend increasing amounts of time at their desks. Make sure that the chair supports the child's back well and is the right size for the type of desk. Position an anglepoise lamp or other desk lamp on or near the desk. If there are younger children in the house, check that no trailing flexes are exposed.

Fix a pinboard above or to the side of the desk and ensure that a bookcase or wall-mounted shelves are nearby for storing reference books. If space is limited, fit castor wheels to a wooden box and tie a rope handle to it. This will become a mobile storage unit for paints or craft activities that need to be out of reach of younger hands, and can double as a small table for drinks and snacks. Combine it with a couple of bean bag cushions so it can serve as a social area when friends come to play.

Use the walls for educational posters such as maps, nature charts or word and number cards. Get your child to help in compiling a photo-collage of all their relatives. Include as many generations as you can find and tell them snippets of family history while you make it.

As this is the age when children formally learn to read and write, make sure there is plenty of book storage and enough pens and pencils in appealing pots, as well as a prominently displayed clock, for learning to tell the time.

Some kind of miniature plan chest or deep, open shelves that are child-height would be useful for storing precious paintings, workbooks and other "projects" such as holiday diaries or collages, photograph albums and family trees.

THE PRIMARY SCHOOL CHILD'S BEDROOM:
FURNISHING SUGGESTIONS

Bed with good mattress

Bedside table and lamp

Homework desk, task light and chair

Dressing table and/or mirror

Additional work/play surface

Hanging storage and drawers or shelves for clothes

Storage for games, sports equipment and craft materials

In our specially created Sailor's Bedroom (see overleaf) an understated homework corner blends easily with the shipshape decor. A simple lamp, a substantial desk and a map of the world all help to concentrate the young mind, while the daylight from the roof window provides good light for working and reading during the daytime.

BEDS AND BEDDING

Bunk beds come into their own with this age group. It is now safe for older children to clamber up to a top bunk to sleep, while the younger members of the age group can enjoy storytime up there before settling down to slumber in the bottom bunk.

Bunks are especially useful if two children are sharing a room or as a permanent guest bed in a single child's room, for cousins and friends to sleep over. Alternatively, visiting children can sleep on a temporary foam mattress and sleeping bag and the mattress can either be stored upright in a wardrobe or tucked under a bed elsewhere in the house.

THE SAILOR'S BEDROOM

This gloriously nautical room (shown on pages 68–9) is packed with decorating ideas on a sailing theme – everything that an enthusiastic pirate or sailor might need for a swashbuckling adventure on the high seas.

Stripes are an enduring design, suitable for boys and girls, and ageless in their application. Use chandler's rope for accessories and let your imagination inspire you to paint seashore scenes, découpage shell motifs and treasure maps, sew laundry kit bags, hang sails or flags from the bedposts or make a bed valance with portholes. Encourage children to come up with their own nautical ideas.

A simple boat made from offcuts of wood or even a cardboard box, combined with scraps of jute or canvas, will delight youngsters. Paint the wood in bright nautical colours and ask your child to come up with a name or number to paint on the hull. Children are always inspired by boats, the sea and the seashore so there will be no shortage of ideas from them.

BOAT BED

Hidden inside this colourful boat, which requires carpentry skills to construct, is a conventional bed frame made from 5 x 5cm (2 x 2in) horizontal timber battens, on which rest wooden slats that support a mattress.

The outer structure is made from thin sheets of MDF cut to shape and screwed to 7.5 x 5cm (3 x 2in) battens. For the sloping edges, the battens were cut at graduating angles; because MDF is quite a pliable material, it curves gently around the battens to form the boat shape. It is easiest to build the sections separately then screw them together *in situ*. The shelf section is slipped over the back end, and screwed in place. Fitting castors to the bottom of the boat bed will allow it to be moved.

To make each sail, cut a right-angled triangle from canvas, and hem all three sides. Insert eyelets at about 12.5cm (5in) intervals down the vertical edge of the mainsail, and lash to the mast with white cord. In the other sail insert eyelets at the corners; using white cord, tie the sail to the top of the mast and to the bottom of the bed. Cut a number (or name) from fusible interfacing, and iron onto the sail.

For the bunting, cut diamond shapes from a variety of striped and plain fabrics. Turn under and press a narrow seam allowance to the wrong side on the raw edges. Fold in half and stitch the triangles down the remaining two edges, wrong sides together, stitching close to the edge, and starting/stopping about 1cm (⅜in) from the top. Thread the bunting onto cord and tie the cord to the top of the mast and the bed.

STRIPY QUILT

Red and blue striped fabrics look great together in a patchwork quilt. Complete with rope hand-holds, the quilt is just what budding sailors need to keep them warm on voyages. Choose a selection of different striped fabrics in nautical reds and blues, then follow the instructions for the Patchwork Cot Quilt on page 40, increasing the size and omitting the small-check and plain borders. When arranging the patchwork pieces, combine squares, rectangles and triangles, and also make some squares with mitred borders (see page 41, step 3). Use different sizes so the effect will be similar to crazy patchwork. When wrapping the backing fabric over the wadding to form an outer border, catch a length of cord into the seam at regular intervals.

SEA-WORTHY COSY CORNER

Whatever your chosen decorative theme, a "real-life" prop or piece of scenery will add a touch of humour and adventure to the scheme. Here, a rowing-boat provides a quiet reading area in a busy boy's bedroom. The idea of climbing aboard a dinghy armed with favourite books and teddies, a cosy quilt and no doubt a few snacks and a torch at night, will be irresistible to any imaginative seven-year-old. Alternatively, you could fence off a corner with chandler's rope and brass poles, and furnish it with squashy bean bags covered in ticking or plain calico.

CUSTOMIZED FLAGS

Ship to shore, the flags shown opposite and on page 75 are versatile adornments for bedheads or wall displays, and will add the finishing touch to a run of bunting or a painting easel. Use them to create a wall display by placing one over another to form a cross shape or as a means of demarcating dens within a room. They could also be used to finish off a wigwam (see page 112) or puppet theatre (page 116).

To make each flag, cut two rectangles from a plain-coloured fabric. Iron on stiff interfacing to the wrong side of one piece. On both pieces press under the edges by 6mm (¼in) all around. Glue a thick wooden skewer or plastic pole to the interfaced piece, then lay the other piece over it, wrong sides together. Topstitch all around the edges using white thread.

Enlarge a motif from the back of the book, or draw a design on tracing paper. We have used a skull-and-crossbones and a seagull, but other possibilities are a reef knot, an anchor, or the child's initials or name. Transfer the design to white felt (and black felt for the seagull's eyes and beak), cut out and glue to the flag.

STOWAWAY STORAGE

Old luggage trunks are versatile and sturdy receptacles for toy debris. No matter how tidy children may or may not be, they accumulate huge quantities of bits and pieces, from discarded teddies to hundreds of fragments of miniature toys. Stow them all away in spacious trunks decorated with nautical motifs and you won't have to worry about containing the clutter for a while.

Either cover the trunks with nautical wallpaper or else découpage ocean-going emblems onto the surface; anything from cut-up old-style world maps to pirate motifs or sailing symbols will be perfect. For extra authenticity, replace any broken handles or straps with rope. (If it looks too new, just soak it in tea to "age" it.) And if the end result looks too good for old toys, use the trunk as a blanket box instead.

Tea chests are another good form of roomy storage if sanded down thoroughly. (Watch out too for nails and sharp corners.) Here, we covered them with wallpaper, painting the rims and edging them with thick sea-blue paper. They can be lined with plain paper or fabric.

WAVY BLINDS

These hand-painted blinds hide away toy clutter in the roof eaves. Make the blinds from a single thickness of cream-coloured canvas, hemming the edges and attaching to the wall with sew-and-stick Velcro. Insert eyelets at the bottom corners and also halfway up, to enable you to fold up the blind so that the waves are still visible. To paint on the waves, use a deep blue fabric paint, having first lightly marked out the shapes with a pencil.

PAINTED MURAL

For the sea in this simple mural, a water-based paint was diluted with water to create the "washy" effect. Mark out your drawing freehand or, if the imagery is complicated, trace it and transfer the tracing to the wall then paint it in. To preserve the finished mural, apply an even coat of acrylic varnish. Children will love to help with a project like this, so choose at least one image they can paint themselves.

NAUTICAL BLIND

A jaunty solution for roof windows in loft conversions, this blind keeps out the light yet looks crisp and stylish when clipped back. Attached by Velcro to the wall itself, the blind also helps to disguise the window recess.

MEASURING

Decide how much of the wall around the window you want the blind to cover. You'll need to cut a piece of fabric twice the length of this area plus 6.5cm (2½in), and the width of the area plus 2.5cm (1in). The dowel will need to be 10cm (4in) shorter than the width of the fabric.

YOU WILL NEED

MAIN FABRIC
MATCHING SEWING THREAD
1.25CM (½IN) DIAMETER DOWELLING
SEW-AND-STICK VELCRO
LARGE EYELETS AND EYELET TOOL
4 CLEATS

1 Fold the piece of fabric in half crosswise, with right sides together, and stitch a 1.25cm (½in) seam down each long side. Turn the fabric right side out and press.

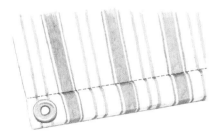

2 Place the length of dowelling inside the blind, along the fold at the bottom, and stitch alongside it to form a casing around the dowel.

3 Apply an eyelet at each bottom corner of the blind, on either side of the length of dowelling.

4 At the top, press under 1.25cm (½in) and then 4cm (1½in). Stitch the sew-on side of the Velcro to this top edge. Stick the self-adhesive side of the Velcro to the wall above the window and attach the blind to this.

5 Screw two cleats to the wall at the bottom and another two cleats three-quarters of the way up on either side. Secure one corner of the blind by slotting the eyelet onto the cleat at the bottom, then fold back the opposite corner and hold it in place on the higher cleat on that side.

DUFFEL BAGS

No self-respecting sailor would be without his kit bag. These durable ticking duffel bags are endlessly useful for laundry, spare shoes or dressing-up clothes, and can also double as overnight bags.

To make a duffel bag, you'll need to cut a circular base, a narrow rectangle and a wider rectangle of fabric. Each rectangle should be as long as the circumference of the circle plus seam allowances. Their width together should add up to the desired height of the bag plus

seam allowances. Cut one rectangle on the lengthwise grain and the other on the crosswise grain. Iron stiff fusible interfacing to the narrow rectangle. Join the rectangles along one long edge, and then join the ends of the piece to form a ring. Hem the top edge, and join the lower edge to the base. Add eyelets around the top edge, then lace the cord through them.

WALL POCKETS

This wall holdall is the perfect solution for tidying away shoes, craft aprons and all the other small, loose paraphernalia children collect effortlessly and in great quantities. Here we have used cream-coloured canvas, but you could use any robust upholstery fabric, patterned or plain, to suit the room. Our pockets are designed with a nautical theme in mind, but you could choose letters, numbers or simple flower or animal shapes as decoration instead.

The instructions here are for a lined and interfaced holdall, which will be sturdy and hard-wearing, but if you use heavy canvas, you will probably not need to line or interface it; you can just hem the edges instead.

Make your pocket system to a size that is appropriate for your wall, and decide what you are going to store in it so that the pockets can be of varying sizes to contain the clutter. Make some pockets work as simple "slots" for thin books, and others with deep pleats to allow chunky shoes to sit happily within. We have used small pockets in the top row, medium-sized ones in the middle row and large ones in the bottom row, with pleats in proportion to the size of the pocket.

YOU WILL NEED

MAIN FABRIC
FABRICS FOR POCKETS AND FOR POCKET DECORATION
MATCHING SEWING THREAD
HEAVYWEIGHT FUSIBLE INTERFACING
STRONG DOWELLING
2 CUP HOOKS

MEASURING

Decide on the size of your finished hanging and draw it out on graph paper. Next, decide on the size and style of the pockets and draw outlines of them onto the plan, calculating how many you need and their exact dimensions. Be sure to allow 5cm (2in) or so above each row of pockets, and a further 4cm (1½in) for the casing at the top of the hanging.

1 Cut out two main pieces of fabric to the overall dimensions, plus 2cm (¾in) all around for seam allowances. Also cut out each pocket, allowing an extra 1.25cm (½in) for seam allowances at the sides and bottom, and 2cm (¾in) at the top. Cut a length of dowelling 10cm (4in) longer than the finished width of the holdall.

2 Cut out a piece of fusible interfacing the same size as the main fabric pieces excluding seam allowances. Iron it onto the back of one fabric piece.

3 Lay the other main fabric piece on top of the interfaced piece, right sides together. Stitch across the top and bottom, taking a 1.25cm (½in) seam and leaving a 20.5cm (8in) opening on one edge. Stitch the same size seam down both sides, leaving the top 2cm

(¾in) of the side seams open just below the top seam.

4 Trim the seams and corners, turn right side out and press. Slipstitch the

opening closed. Topstitch 2cm (¾in) from the top edge to form a casing for the dowel.

5 Cut out the pieces of fabric for the pocket decoration, turn under a 3mm (⅛in) hem on each edge and press. Attach the decoration to each pocket by topstitching close to the edges.

6 Press under 6mm (¼in) then 1.25cm (½in) on the top edge of each pocket; stitch. Press under 1.25cm (½in) on the side and bottom edges.

7 Pin all the pockets onto the interfaced side of the holdall, forming

two pleats on the bottom edge of each. Topstitch around the side and bottom edges of each pocket.

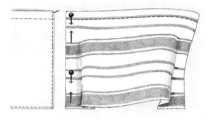

8 Slot the dowel through the casing at the top so that the ends extend beyond the side edges by 5cm (2in). Hang the holdall from cup hooks screwed into the wall on either side.

THE LITTLE PRINCESS'S ROOM

Our Little Princess's room has been inspired by the clean lines of traditional Scandinavian design, especially the beautiful 19th-century watercolours by Carl Larsson of his own daughter's bedroom at his home in Sweden. The Little Princess's room was designed to satisfy a young girl's yearning for a totally pink room (without having to make it so pink that she would grow out of it in a year). The fresh-looking checks and small floral prints make a classic combination in subtle pink tones, without being too sugary sweet.

The idea of an enclosed bed incorporating some storage space is irresistible to most young girls. Here, we echoed the bed pelmet with the window treatment. The floorboards were painted white to keep the room bright, while the painted furniture ensures that the room remains feminine.

The furnishings are echoed inside the dolls' house – a project a young girl might enjoy doing herself, while learning basic sewing skills.

Very feminine but not overdone, this delicately decorated Little Princess's Bedroom is the epitome of many young girls' aspirations. Soft shades of rose pink, cosy corners and pretty painted furniture almost belong to another age, and combine to form a timeless scheme for a little girl's fairy tale room. Scallop-edged pelmets set off the window and bed curtains.

YOU WILL NEED

LINING PAPER

BLUE, BLUE-GREEN AND PINK EMULSION
PAINT

MATT EMULSION GLAZE

LOW-TACK MASKING TAPE

BORDER ADHESIVE

1 Unroll the paper and cut to a depth of about 30cm (12in) and a length of about 3m (10ft).

STENCILLED WALLPAPER BORDER

This fine scroll-design border has a faded elegance born of its eau-de-nil, salmon-pink and biscuit colour combination. Stencilled directly onto lining paper whose texture is slightly uneven, it is a perfect finishing touch for the room's gentle feeling of antiquity.

2 Trace the template at the back of the book, and transfer to stencil card or acetate. Cut out the stencil. Use low-tack masking tape to stick the stencil to the lining paper. First stencil in sky blue paint sparingly all along the length of the border. Leave the paint to dry, then replace the stencil in each position and apply blue-green paint sparingly. Stencilling all one colour and then replacing the stencil, rather than doing both colours before repositioning it, creates an attractive, slightly out-of-register effect, adding an interesting softness to the edges. You can accentuate the effect by using a sponge rather than a brush to apply the paint, giving a dappled texture.

3 Draw a faint pencil line 2.5cm (1in) in from the top and bottom edges. (Or use low-tack masking tape to help you paint straight, but peel it off carefully.) Paint on the pink colour with a flat 2.5cm (1in) wide brush. Seal with a matt emulsion glaze.

4 To mount the border, apply border adhesive, folding the paper concertina-fashion, then fix to the wall.

PAINTED DECORATION

By the age of about eight, girls have usually developed a fascination with dressing tables, and this painted wooden one has the requisite prettiness without the frills and furbelows. The hand-painted decoration echoes the scroll pattern and the pink/green colours of the wallpaper border.

These subtle decorative extras, with their soft colours echoed in the stencilled border running around the walls of the room, provide a pleasing harmony with the off-white painted floorboards – clean, fresh and simple as only Scandinavian style can be.

Subtle pink scrolls are also painted onto the wardrobe door (see left), whose panels feature a children's novelty print wallpaper, pasted on with PVA glue. The white background of the paper on the white door makes the images resemble hand-painting.

Another method of achieving a hand-painted look without actually being able to draw was used on the small cupboard next to the fireplace (opposite). The characters were traced from children's illustrations and enlarged on a photocopier; the outlines were then transferred to the panels of the cupboard and painted in by hand.

An even easier method was used on the fireplace itself: photocopies of the figures were simply cut out and stuck onto the panels then hand-painted and sealed with a matt emulsion glaze.

The decoration was applied over a dusky pink colourwash edged with eau-de-nil on the fireplace, and over shades of biscuit framed by Gustavian blue and ice pink on the cupboard. For a translucent colourwash such as this, dilute water-based paint until it gives only a light tracing of colour on your chosen surface. Apply more than one coat if necessary.

DOLLS' HOUSE

Dolls' houses have an enduring and fascinating charm. Their miniature worlds provide endless possibilities for everyone, from three-year-olds to adults. Unlike real homes, the rooms can be redecorated as often as you like. A child can have fun re-upholstering a sofa, changing the window coverings or renewing the wallpaper – and will be able to complete it before they grow tired of the job. The furnishings can echo those of their own bedroom, as here, or else be totally one-off in style.

Make tiny cushions and bolsters and stuff them with cotton wool or kapok. Hang "proper" curtains (fringing the lower edges by removing a few horizontal threads) then hold them back with tiebacks made from narrow ribbon. Cut little bedcovers from fabric bearing motifs of the right scale. Use pinking shears to cut out tablecloths from gingham.

SCALLOPED PELMET, CURTAINS AND TIEBACKS

These simple curtains and coordinating scallop-edged pelmet lend an air of quiet sophistication to a young girl's room. The curtains are unlined to allow the light to filter through, adding to the airiness of the room. The scalloped edge of the pelmet can be piped or left plain. Combined with matching tiebacks, the sleek and tailored pelmet adds a smart informality to the room.

YOU WILL NEED

FABRIC FOR CURTAINS

FABRIC FOR PELMET AND TIEBACKS

PLAIN FABRIC OR BIAS BINDING FOR PIPING

MATCHING SEWING THREAD

PIPING CORD

HEADING TAPE

FUSIBLE INTERFACING

SEW-AND-STICK VELCRO

4 BRASS RINGS

2 CUP HOOKS

MEASURING

Curtains

The fullness of the curtains will depend upon the heading tape you choose. Standard heading tape requires 1½ to 2 times the width, pinch pleat tape 2 times and pencil pleat tape 3 times the width. Therefore, for the width of the curtains, multiply this number times the width of the track, plus 7.5cm (3in) for the side hems. Divide this by the width of the fabric, and round up to get the number of widths you will need.

For the length of each drop of the curtain fabric, measure from the track to the desired length and add the depth of the heading tape plus 12.5cm (5in) for the bottom hem.

For the total amount of fabric you'll need, multiply the length of each drop by the number of widths. If the fabric is patterned, add the depth of one extra pattern repeat per fabric width after the first width.

Pelmet

For the fabric width, measure the width of your pelmet board (including the distance around the ends if you wish the pelmet to continue around the corners), and add 2.5cm (1in) for seam allowances. The depth of the pelmet is up to you, but the finished length of pelmets like this is generally about one-sixth the length of the curtains. Your pelmet fabric needs to be this depth plus 2.5cm (1in). Cut two pieces of fabric to these dimensions.

Tiebacks

To decide the length of your tiebacks, hold a tape measure around the curtain when it is pulled back. Add 2.5cm (1in) to this length for seam allowances. Experiment with the height. Sometimes tiebacks are fixed about two-thirds of the way down the curtain, other times fairly high up.

Curtains

1 Cut out enough fabric widths for each curtain, matching any pattern all the way across. Join the widths, right sides together, taking 1.25cm (½in) seams and matching the pattern. If your window requires an odd number of fabric widths, use a half width on each curtain and position it on the outside edge rather than the leading (inside) edge.

2 Press under 5mm (¼in) and then 7cm (2¾in) on each side edge. Stitch. Measure the depth of your heading tape and turn down this amount at the top; press.

3 Position the heading tape on the wrong side just inside the folded top edge. Knot the two cords together on the leading edge of each curtain and turn under the end of the tape. Stitch across the end and along both edges, stitching in the same direction each time. At the outside edge, turn under the end of the tape, and stitch, being careful to keep the cords free.

4 On the bottom edge, turn under 5mm (¼in) and then 12cm (4¾in). Hand sew the hem in place.

5 Pull up the cords on the heading tape to form narrow pleats. When the curtain is the correct width, knot the cords together. (Do not cut them off.) Insert hooks behind each pleat, and hang from the track.

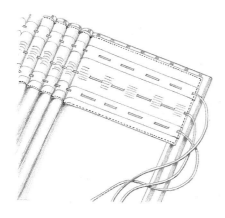

Pelmet

1 If you do not already have a pelmet board, fit one 5–8cm (2–3in) above the window frame so it projects 5cm (2in) beyond each end of the curtain rail.

2 Cut a strip of fusible interfacing to the dimensions of the pelmet fabric excluding the seam allowances. Following the manufacturer's instructions, iron the fusible interfacing to the wrong side of one fabric piece, along one edge.

3 Place the interfaced fabric on a flat surface, interfacing side uppermost. Draw around a plate to create a scalloped edge 1cm (⅜in) inside the lower edge, leaving a gap of 1cm (⅜in) at each end. Also leave a gap of this size between semicircles if you plan to

pipe the edge. Hand tack along the marked line so the scalloped line will be visible from the right side.

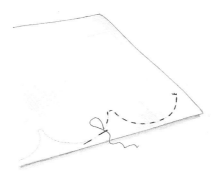

4 If you are using fabric rather than purchased bias binding for the piping, cut strips of the plain fabric on the bias. (Work out the width the strips should be by wrapping the fabric around the piping cord and pinning it next to the cord. Add two 1cm (⅜in) seam allowances to this distance.) Join the ends of the bias strips on the straight grain, then wrap the binding around the piping cord. Tack the binding close to the cord.

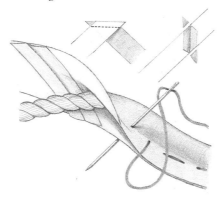

5 Pin the piping along the tacked scalloped line on the right side of the fabric, as shown, clipping into the seam allowances on the curves. Tack.

Place the other piece of fabric on top, right sides together, sandwiching the piping between. Stitch along the scalloped line, continuing across each end with a 1cm (⅜in) seam. Trim the seams and corners. Turn right side out and press. Turn in 1cm (⅜in) on the raw edges at the top; press and tack.

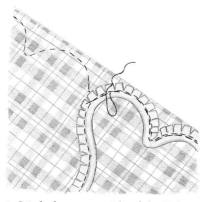

6 Stitch the sew-on side of the Velcro along the top edge of the pelmet at the back. Remove the tacking. Stick the self-adhesive side of the Velcro to the pelmet board. Fix the pelmet in place.

Tiebacks

1 To draw up a crescent-shaped pattern, mark on a piece of paper a strip that is half the tieback length measurement by 10cm (4in) wide. Curve both sides at the bottom so that one end is narrowed to 4cm (1½in). Cut out this pattern.

2 Fold a piece of fabric in half on the straight grain and place the wide end of the pattern against the fold. Cut out, adding a 1.25cm (½in) seam allowance on the cut edges. Repeat for a second piece of fabric, but in reverse. Cut two more fabric pieces in the same way for the other tieback.

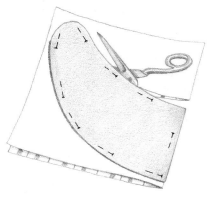

3 Using the template you have made, cut out a piece of fusible stiff interfacing for each tieback, omitting the seam allowance. Fuse each to the wrong side of one fabric piece.

4 Make piping as for the pelmet (step 4), and tack all around the seamline on the right side of one tieback,.

5 With right sides together, join the interfaced and uninterfaced fabric pieces, taking a 1.25cm (½in) seam and leaving an opening. Trim the seam, turn right side out and press. Slipstitch the opening. Repeat for other tieback.

6 Blanket stitch a ring centrally at each end on the wrong side so that it projects slightly beyond the fabric. Hook each tieback's pair of rings onto a cup hook on the wall.

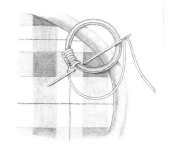

BED HANGINGS

This delightful four-poster bed is both a retreat and a reading area rolled into one. The bed frame, which simply slots over a divan bed, is made in much the same way as the bed frame on page 56 (and, like it, requires carpentry skills), but an MDF ceiling is fixed to the top and lined with fabric. After the bed frame has been constructed, the integral shelf unit is slipped into one end and screwed on. The outer curtains are hooked onto a rail attached to the frame so that they can be fully opened and closed. The pelmet is stuck with Velcro to a strip of hardboard fixed in front of the curtain rail.

Make the two outer curtains as for the window curtains. For the inner curtains, join enough widths to make one very wide curtain that will cover the wall on the far side and at the end behind the bedhead. Stitch adhesive-backed pencil-pleat heading tape to the top, remove the backing and stick to the bed frame.

Make the pelmet as for the window pelmet, piping the scalloped edge or not, as you wish.

The valance around the bed (see page 82) incorporates a single inverted pleat, creating a tailored look that complements the gathered window curtains in the same striped fabric.

CHAPTER SIX

The Teenage Years

When children enter the teenage years, their increased awareness of themselves and their surroundings may mean that you have very little say in the decoration of their rooms, other than to provide financial support for any furnishing requirements.

You can help smooth the transition from child to young adult by allowing a teenager's room to reflect their own interests and personality. If all they want to do is lie around on cushions drinking coffee and strumming a guitar instead of indulging in regular exercise, then let them create a room that is a comfortable place for them to retreat to when the going gets tough. Since teenagers, when at home, spend much more time in their own rooms than younger children do, their space should really be their own.

For studious types, a built-in desk with fabric curtains to hide homework would be ideal, while sporty types would find a tall cupboard for sports equipment essential. Suggest rather than impose decorative changes, but be on hand to help out when required. If your offspring suddenly develop a passion for sewing, painting woodwork or metalwork, take care not to shun the creative urge for fear of a few gouges out of the wall, a paint-spattered floor or a damaged sewing machine. Enthusiasm is all at this age.

A den that can be treated as a home within a home is the kind of room to which most teenagers aspire, and our Teenage Den (see page 97) provides a space they can call their own (and no doubt retire to at every available opportunity). Clothes, books, sports equipment and home entertainment systems are all squeezed into this canopied room.

THE IDEAL BEDROOM

For most teenagers, the perfect bedroom would include furniture, equipment and furnishings reminiscent of a studio apartment. It would be spacious, with not too much cumbersome furniture, but with plenty of improvised pieces to house equipment such as a computer, a music system and vast quantities of CDs and tapes, a work desk and some musical instruments.

No self-respecting young adult would be without a social space for entertaining friends, so beds are not so much beds as communal daybeds, strewn with cushions, while sofas and armchairs can be draped with throws (and also, quite possibly, the contents of the wardrobe, which can often be found spread, inexplicably, over all available surfaces).

FURNITURE NEEDS

Whereas a busy 12-year-old will relish an organized, modular desk area plus shelving, a 16-year-old may well wish to demonstrate their independence by finding a battered storage cabinet in a junkyard and transforming it into a mobile TV trolley, by painting it and replacing

the door. While an active 10-year-old will enjoy having tennis racquets and cricket bats neatly stacked in a cupboard or under the bed, an older teenager is more likely to toss them carelessly into whichever large receptacle is nearest the door.

Plan for this dramatic transition by investing in a few large containers such as wicker baskets, aluminium dustbins, large wall-mounted shelves or additional chests of drawers. Leave them unpainted, or strip existing pieces whose colours may now be inappropriate, and let your teenager decide on a colour scheme. This way you cannot be blamed for a "boring" result – although you will undoubtedly be enlisted into a colour-altering operation if anything does not turn out as planned.

Informal Indian fabrics and rich chenilles on scatter cushions and at the window add to the atmosphere of our Teenage Den (see pages 93 and 97). With a television as a focal point, this is certainly no Homework Corner.

An easy chair, enlivened with generous, bold-patterned cushions, can provide a focal point for the room's decoration. If the ceilings are high and strong, a hammock suspended from sturdy metal hooks fixed to a joist is an ideal place for teenage daydreaming and future-planning, offering a great escape from the work desk and exam pressures.

Define a social area by placing floor cushions on top of painted wooden pallets to form a low platform. Range them around a low coffee table piled with magazines and candles for the ultimate in cool entertaining.

A kettle and some mugs suspended from cup hooks can form a mini-kitchen. Separate it from the work or sleep area by a wicker screen.

If the size of the room dictates that there is space only for a bed, try removing the bedhead and converting the sleeping area into a daybed/sofa by piling it high with large cushions, generous bolsters and drapes and throws. Attach a simple canopy above it for an enclosed effect. Positioning it in an alcove will also help it to not look like a bed.

Provide an ample-sized desk for homework. It can even be improvised from a door placed on two trestles, which will allow some flexibility in the layout of the room. Pinboards are still important; repaint existing ones, or devote the upper half of one wall to a strip of corkboard. Make sure that the computer is placed away from direct light so that there is no problem with glare. Lighting should be localized and effective for late-night studying.

DECORATING

Children of this age will certainly be capable of performing nearly any decorating task. Persuading them that it will be fun to do may be more tricky. However, spur on their enthusiasm with a trip to the shops to select fabric and accessories. Discuss ideas for making the room more of a space for one-room living than a bedroom.

Floor cushions are a good starting point for a decorating scheme. Choosing fabric for these may lead to some bold ideas for window treatments and bedlinen elsewhere in the room. A cabina, which will house cricket bats, tennis racquets and oars as well as a large amount of clutter, is another opportunity for a swathe of bold colour.

While a traditional floral chintz may be spurned during the teenage years, a rich purple or burgundy plain fabric, jazzed up with checked or stripy floor cushions could look dramatic and be well received. Fabric can be used in bed hangings, too. Girls may prefer a bed canopy for a hint of romance: white muslin or plain damask would both work well.

At this age, wallpaper comes into its own, as it is less likely to be scuffed and marked than painted walls. A pretty border with a vivid striped wallpaper, or a combination of dark colours and a subtle border, would suit a girl or a boy respectively, although girls may also prefer darker colours, for a study-like atmosphere.

STORAGE

Teenagers tend to accumulate clutter of a different sort from younger children. Rather than toys and their tiny components, there will be plenty of paper to store. Notebooks of poems, looseleaf binders crammed with school notes and projects, textbooks and reference works will all need homes. Bookshelves are often far too small, having seemingly been designed for nothing but paperbacks. Try altering any existing wall-mounted shelves or consider devoting an entire wall to deep, open shelves. Make a virtue of larger items such as rucksacks, cricket paraphernalia and rugby footballs, displaying them boldly atop shelves or in a sturdy fisherman's net suspended from the ceiling or a strong metal wall peg.

Whereas you may have got away with a small wardrobe and a chest of drawers for clothes storage up to now, the teenage years usually mark a dramatic increase in the quantity of clothes, be they diaphanous dresses, myriad pairs of rugged, aged jeans or huge volumes of T-shirts. Consider investing in a large, freestanding wardrobe, or adapt any existing pigeon-hole shelves to house folded clothes.

As well as the fabric-covered cabina already mentioned, which can hold large amounts of clutter in a relatively small space, another option is a trunk on castors – it can double as a clothes store and low table.

A change in room layout can often mark the transition from one stage of childhood to the next. One way of providing extra storage is to move the bed into the centre of the room and create a mock bedhead by arranging four chests of drawers or cupboards around it in a U-shape. This not only encloses the bed but also provides walk-around storage and a surface for table lamps, decorative pieces and piles of reading matter. Or create a walk-in dressing area behind the bed rather than devoting a whole wall to a built-in wardrobe.

DETAILS

Mirrors play an important part in the lives of teenagers, so make a feature of them and place them in prominent positions. Self-adhesive fabric or plastic can be used to cover plain wooden frames, or frames can be painted to match pinboards or woodwork elsewhere in the room. Surround the mirror with pegs on which brushes, combs, hairdryers and jewellery can be displayed and stored. This minimizes the effort involved in keeping the room tidy. Laundry also becomes important to a teenager – or at least having somewhere to put clothes ready for the wash does. Provide a deep linen basket or metal dustbin, depending on the style of room. Confine it to a corner, possibly disguised with a screen, and empty when necessary. Your progeny certainly won't remember to, unless desperate for something to do.

THE TEENAGER'S ROOM: SUGGESTED FURNISHINGS

Bed, possibly with storage underneath

Large wardrobe or built-in storage for clothes

Study desk

Shelving for school files

Table/work station for computer

Home entertainment/hi-fi/TV storage

Scatter cushions and low table

Futon or daybed with throws

Coat-rack and hooks

Large pinboard or cork-lined wall

THE TEENAGE DEN

For those years when children are transmuting into young adults, a flexible approach to furnishing is called for. Our Teenage Den (shown on pages 92–3) is the sort of room teenagers would themselves choose. The fabric is inexpensive, and it is arranged over the bed and at the window in quick, easy to hang ways, for maximum impact with minimum effort.

SIMPLE WINDOW TREATMENTS

Lengths of muslin in vibrant shades of Kashmir red and saffron yellow are pinned with strong drawing pins to the window frames of our Teenage Den, one overlapping the other so they give the sunlight streaming through them a summery glow even on the coldest of days. Here, they are both caught back on one side with wrought-iron tiebacks.

Another way to create an informal effect is to drape layers of muslin in different colours or a mixture of plain and patterned fabrics over a metal or wooden pole. They can be finished off with a fabric bow tieback, a tassel or rope. Or tie a single muslin curtain to a pole in a variation of our Amazon curtains (page 64) and gather in the middle with a huge muslin sash.

CLEVER IMPROVISATION

An airy, informal arrangement of furniture and fabric makes this room seem as if anything can happen with the decoration. The bed canopy is easily replaceable or movable, as are the window treatments, which are simply pinned on, and the bedhead on castors.

Note the cheap secondhand metal cabinet, easily painted by the teenager, and perfect for storing sports equipment. The low futon bed with its colourful bedspread and bolster can double as an ethnic sofa.

BED CANOPY

To make a simple bed canopy like the one on the left, take a length of lightweight fabric which has a natural sympathy with the bed covering. Hem each long edge (unless it is the selvage) and both ends. Insert two screw eyes into the ceiling above where each end of the canopy will be, and run a sturdy length of yachting wire between each pair of screw eyes. Now simply drape the fabric over the two wires. Knot the draped ends or attach fringing, braid or contrasting binding. To coordinate the look, use the same fabric for bolster or scatter cushion covers or for binding the edges of curtains.

DECORATING THE BED

In teenagers' rooms, because the bed will often double as a daytime and evening lounging area, it's much appreciated if you make it comfortable by adding generous bolsters, soft oversized cushions and interesting throws.

Some kind of canopy or enclosure will increase the sense of privacy, so you might consider constructing a more adult version of the bedframe in the Owl and the Pussycat room (see page 53). Instead of making a wooden punched pelmet, drape the horizontal timbers with long lengths of fabric such as blue muslin, or make curtains with tab or eyelet headings. The more fabric you use, the more lavish it will look.

BEDHEAD WITH STORAGE

Customized furniture is one way of accommodating the teenager's love of informality while still allowing for some decoration. The bed in our Teenager's Den (see pages 98–9), with its L-shaped bedhead, is particularly versatile, because it can be positioned as it has been there, like an island, or it can be placed with the other side of the bed up against a wall.

The bedhead is simple to construct using two existing pieces of bedroom furniture: a chest of drawers and a deep cupboard. Placed with the storage areas facing outwards, they are held together with a sheet of 1.25cm (½in) thick MDF (medium-density fibreboard) screwed to the top and down each of the inward-facing surfaces. Fixing castors to each corner allows the whole unit to be transported around the room if required.

Paint the MDF and, if you wish, decorate it with stencilling, découpage or stamping techniques.

Alternatively, for a softer effect, drape the unit with fabric and pile it high with boxes covered in a coordinating fabric.

FUTON

Futons are popular with teenagers, either to sleep on themselves or to use as spare beds. Adults, it must be said, often cannot understand what the attraction is, as futons do tend to be less soft than conventional beds, and take some getting used to. These firm mattresses can be supported on a low slatted wood base, as here, or used on the floor and then rolled up during the day. When the mattress is rolled up halfway, the built-in backrest makes it an ideal spot for relaxing. This futon, which is about 10cm (4in) thick, is made from flock wadding (available from upholsterers) and is hand-tufted at regular intervals.

YOU WILL NEED

COTTON FABRIC
MATCHING SEWING THREAD
2.5CM- (1IN-) THICK FLOCK WADDING
UPHOLSTERER'S NEEDLE
TWINE

1 Cut out two pieces of fabric to the desired length of the futon plus 9cm (3½in) and the desired width plus 9cm (3½in). Cut four layers of wadding, each to the desired dimensions (without adding extra).

2 The fabric covering is made first. With right sides together, join both long edges with 2cm (¾in) seams but leave a central opening in one of these seams for most of the length.

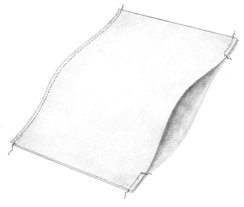

3 Refold the fabric so the seams run down the centre of each side, then stitch a 2cm (¾in) seam across each end. Press the seams open.

4 At each corner, separate the front and back, centring the seam. Mark a 10cm (4in) long line across the corner, pin and stitch through both layers. Do not trim the seam. When all four corners have been stitched, turn the cover right side out.

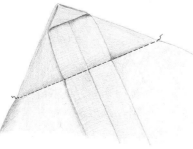

5 Insert the layers of wadding through the centre back opening. Slipstitch the opening closed, using a double length of thread and placing the stitches very close together.

6 Mark the positions of the tufts so they are about 25cm (10in) apart, and staggered. Thread the upholsterer's needle with a double or quadruple length of twine. Take the needle through from front to back, leaving 10cm (4in) long ends. Bring the needle back to the front, to make a 2.5cm (1in) wide stitch. Tie the ends of twine in a firm reef knot, then trim them to 6.5cm (2½in).

101

BOLSTERS

Long bolsters are ideal for relaxing on, whether used on a low bed or futon, or combined with cushions of other shapes and sizes. The long lines of the bolster mean that striped fabrics are especially suitable. If the stripe or pattern is quite strong, a tailored bolster with a zip, like the one shown on page 98-99, generally works best. If you prefer it to be a little less plain, you can pipe the ends.

1 Cut a piece of fabric as long as the bolster plus 4cm (1½in), and as wide as the circumference of the bolster plus 4cm (1¼in). Cut two circles from the fabric, with the diameter of each equal to the diameter of the bolster plus 4cm (1½in).

2 With right sides together, fold the fabric in half and stitch along the length, taking a 2cm (¾in) seam but machine tacking rather than stitching where the zip will be inserted. Insert the zip, then remove the tacking and open the zip.

3 With right sides together, pin each end to a circle. Stitch, taking a 2cm (¾in) seam and clipping into the seam allowance on the curves. Turn right side out through the zip opening and insert the bolster pad.

STUDY AREA

Make doing homework more appealing by paying some attention to the study area. Create a good-sized desk using simple trestles with a door laid on top. Site it next to some equally functional, no-nonsense shelving. Or, for a less streamlined look, disguise cluttered open shelves with fabric drapes, and add comfort to work chairs with cushions. Decorate simple cork noticeboards with painted borders or fabric edging.

If there is a television, incorporate it into the room by placing it on a fabric-draped low table, or fit it on a swivel arm so it can "disappear" into a curtained alcove when study time takes over. Surround it with floor cushions for informal viewing.

CHAPTER SEVEN

Beyond the Bedroom

The presence of children in a home should be celebrated rather than disguised, although their propensity to spread toys, belongings and friends to all corners of the dwelling can be alarming for those of an orderly tendency.

Once their bedrooms become their havens, children like to use other parts of the house – and garden – for different activities. It is a good idea to anticipate which spaces will become dens, entertainment areas or lounging-around sites and plan them accordingly. Children love nothing better than cosy nooks and crannies in which to hide or indulge their imaginations with make-believe.

By devoting another space in the house to children's activities you will create an additional gathering place which will relieve pressure on other busy parts of the home. It should also enable you to preserve at least one room that is strictly for the grown-ups.

If you are short of additional space, think about providing an extra play area, seating or storage under the stairs, in an underused alcove, in the hallway or on the landing. Use room dividers in a large room to separate off a toy storage space for youngsters or a leisure area for older children.

Outside, there is often considerable scope for coping with overflow from indoors. Garden sheds, garden rooms or conservatories added onto the side of the house and freestanding playhouses are all ways of making room for children.

A playroom can be conjured up from any available space in the home – off a kitchen or living room is ideal. In our Creative Play Room (page 110) an open doorway has been transformed into a puppet theatre, while a wigwam provides a place to hide or a special location for indoor picnics.

OUTDOORS

Playhouses, rope ladders and swings, sandpits, miniature gardens and paddling pools are all an intrinsic part of childhood. Treehouses are the scene of many a secret assignment planned during lunchtime picnics, where torches and binoculars, spy notebooks and bird-spotting are *de rigueur.*

Playhouses in whatever form are even more fun in the garden than indoors. The wigwam in our Creative Play Room (page 112) can be set up anywhere, inside or out. Or create a canopied den by draping fabric over beanpoles; bold florals will conjure up a country garden, and stripy canvas a sense of the seaside.

A garden shed could double as a playhouse: stow away all dangerous equipment and put pretty gingham curtains with bow tiebacks on the windows. Add a couple of wicker hampers and a cane chair, and your children will remember their pastoral hide-away for ever.

KITCHENS

Pre-school children, especially, love being around you in the kitchen. It's generally when you are preparing for a dinner party that they want to embark on an epic artwork involving the entire contents of the crafts cupboard and a few discarded household items. With a large table and the right equipment, you will be able to get on in small doses while keeping a supervisory eye on their artistic endeavours.

Now that the kitchens is, more often than not, the most lived-in room of the home, it makes sense to devote some space here to children's activities. It is safest if the cooking and food preparation part of the kitchen is placed at one end, or in one corner, while a table for meals and other practical pursuits is at the other end. Provide some form of toy storage, a miniature table and chairs, and "wet play" space for painting, working with play dough and cutting and sticking. If you have a large window, consider building a window seat with a hinged lid to hide painting equipment and toys. Or construct some pigeon-hole shelving for toy and craft materials storage, and hang a fabric blind in front of it to disguise the contents.

However you organize the space when the children are young, it can be adapted as they grow. The same space can be given over to an easy chair and some books, a fold-down work desk and chair, or a home entertainment area complete with television and miniature hi-fi system on a swivel arm.

Encourage tidiness at an early age by providing child-height hooks and pegs for storing coats, hats, cardigans and painting aprons.

A wigwam is a neat alternative to the more usual Wendy house. It will inspire many dressing-up games as well as making the transition from indoors to garden very easily.

LIVING ROOMS

However much you may wish to preserve the living room as the grown-up room of the house, children do tend to congregate here If you decide that there really is nowhere else to accommodate additional toys and games, then there are ways of incorporating youthful possessions into the scheme of things without the room looking like an overstocked toy shop.

Try dividing off a corner of the room with a fabric or wicker screen to hide baskets of toys and board games. Computers can be housed on a roll-out trolley in an armoire or built-in cupboard, with children's video and cassette tapes. Store books on low shelves, within easy reach of children.

If the room is large enough, devote one end or one corner of the room to the children and demarcate it by painting it a different colour or by pasting a border at dado height. Alternatively, screen off the area with curtains or separate it with a screen, sofa or table.

In a living room where all members of the family will inevitably gather, certain things are best avoided while children are young. Among them are cream or white sofas and carpets and glass-topped tables. Ceramics, antiques and fine upholstery simply will not survive the energetic games of gregarious five-year-olds. However strict you are about insisting on stockinged feet and banning food and drink from the living room, the very speed at which children charge around when they have friends to play would make breakages inevitable. It is far safer, for your blood pressure and their peace of mind, to ensure that sofas and chairs have loose covers, coffee tables are kept simple and free of ornaments (and out of the way when toddlers are about) and precious lamps have their flexes hidden. Make sure treasured china is well out of reach, together with any other highly prized objects. Keep your serious Persian carpet or your needlepoint upholstery for when the children have left home.

On the walls, very pale colour schemes will get dirty more quickly than richer colours. On windows, ensure that your curtain rails are fixed firmly in position. Who doesn't remember having a quick swing on the curtains when the adults were out of the room?

There is something very reassuring about generously pleated curtains in a living room. Pelmets and tiebacks will lend an air of traditional domesticity. Checked throws will help protect sofas during the daytime rough-and-tumble, then at night fold them up or drape them and enjoy some pristine seating.

Dining chairs and an old rug make an excellent basis for a makeshift playhouse. Children invariably prefer imaginary games such as this to the latest fad board game, so try to be flexible if the younger generation want to reorganize the layout of the room temporarily.

One advantage of being fairly relaxed about your furnishings is that you will not need to fret about anything valuable being ruined. And you will at least be guaranteed some peace while the room is transformed into a Swiss Family Robinson home.

PLAYROOMS

If you have the space, creating a playroom out of one part of the kitchen or a small box room off the living room or a bedroom is an ideal way to allow children the freedom to spread out their toys and activities undisturbed by the rigours of routine. It will mean less space in their bedroom devoted to storage, and for families of two or more children, a place where the youngsters can gather together.

You don't need a massive home with lots of spare rooms. Any small room can be adapted as a playroom and can also incorporate other activities. If equipped with a sofa bed and chest of drawers it can double as a guest room. With a small desk and adequate task lighting it can also be used as a sewing room or study – especially useful if you have teenagers and young children at home. As an adjunct to a kitchen or in an underused dining room, a playroom forms an extension of the heart of the home and allows you to watch over small ones as they play and you get on with chores.

When decorating a playroom, avoid making the more permanent furnishings look too childish – especially if the room will double as a study or guest room.

If you supply childlike decor in the form of posters or soft toys suspended in mock hammocks, and stacking boxes or baskets crammed with toys, then you can choose wall, window and floor coverings that will appeal to all ages. However, avoid carpet if your children are quite young, and choose instead a large rug, placed over a non-slip mat.

An old chimneybreast in our Creative Play Room (overleaf) provides a cosy alcove for miniature furniture, while adjacent cupboards are painted in a harlequin style.

From a safety point of view, check that you have enough electrical sockets, so you can avoid trailing flexes. Place some sockets midway up the wall if a computer is to be installed at some point. Protect sockets with child-proof covers.

A comfortable playroom is one that any member of the family will like to use for time out, while watching the little ones play or chatting with teenagers about homework problems. It provides an extra family room where a range of activities can take place.

THE CREATIVE PLAY ROOM

As every child knows, learning is fun when it is through creative play. This cheerful playroom (shown in full on pages 104–5) offers exactly that. Painted numbers and letters decorate the walls and playthings, and there is plenty of opportunity for stimulating activities, ranging from games and play-acting to stories and craft work. There is also ample storage, all of it attractive and colourful.

COLOUR-BY-NUMBER WALLS

Letters and numbers are enormously interesting to children of this age. Not only are they of great value educationally, but they also have infinite decorative applications. You can stencil names onto walls or furniture, paint numbers directly onto a floor for an instant games area or form a border at chair-rail height on a wall.

Here, letters and numbers have been hand-painted more or less at random on the yellow colourwashed walls. Simply trace the letters and numerals at the back of the book, transfer to the wall and then paint them in. Or, if you aren't confident about hand-painting, use the templates to make stencils.

On one area of wall at the end of the room, we used a deeper yellow for the background, framing this with an even darker shade of yellow and a fine orange line. At the top, the numbers form a frieze. Defining a specific part of the wall in this way creates a giant display area that is just right for those pictures proudly brought home from nursery school.

To make the painted walls easy to clean, protect them with a matt emulsion glaze.

DIAMOND DESIGN CUPBOARDS

Abstract or geometric shapes combine well with letter and number motifs and have been used to decorate the cupboards in this playroom in various ways, all using diluted emulsion paint in blues and yellows.

On the wide cupboard door shown on the far right of the photograph above, the diamonds are created by first washing the full panel in pale blue, then stencilling yellow diamond shapes on the raised central portion of each border. Using a sponge rather than a brush to stencil creates an uneven look that goes well with the

colourwashing. The architrave is painted in the same pale blue, and everything protected with matt acrylic varnish.

On the narrow cupboard door shown on the left of the photograph on page 109, blue diamonds have been stencilled onto yellow panels, again using a sponge, with the mouldings and the door frame picked out in blue.

The inside of the cupboard door, which is shown above, has been given a similar treatment, but alternate diamonds are stencilled (with a sponge) in a deeper yellow, then outlined by hand in blue, and varnished.

The inside of the cupboard itself has hand-painted harlequin diamonds which have been sealed with matt emulsion glaze.

WIGWAM

This wigwam can be used indoors or out and is just the place for a secret pow-wow, a quiet picnic or private reading. Fairly simple to make, it will stimulate children's imaginations and quickly become a favourite plaything.

YOU WILL NEED

STRONG COTTON FABRIC SUCH AS CANVAS
OR CALICO

MATCHING SEWING THREAD

6 GARDEN CANES,
EACH ABOUT 2M (6FT 6IN) LONG

6MM (¼IN) WIDE ROPE

2CM (¾IN) WIDE PETERSHAM RIBBON

ACRYLIC PAINT

MEASURING

Assemble your canes and tie them together with a rope to form the basic wigwam structure. Measure the canes, adding 2.5cm (1in) for hems, and use this measurement as a radius for drawing a semicircle for the cover.

1 Tie a pencil to a piece of string the length of your radius. Hold the other end in place and use the string to draw a semicircle on newspaper; cut out the pattern. Join widths of fabric as necessary to make a large enough piece, then draw around the pattern and cut out the semicircle from fabric.

2 At the centre of the straight edge, draw and cut out a semicircle large enough to fit around the top of the tied poles – probably about 15cm (6in) across). Turn under a 1.25cm (½in) double hem on all edges.

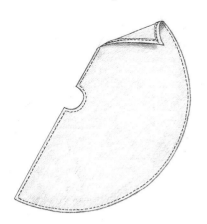

3 Paint, stencil or stamp your chosen designs onto the canvas. Here we used children's hand prints and stencilled numbers and letters.

4 Place the canvas over the canes, with the front opening positioned centrally between two canes. One side will overlap the other.

5 Cut the ribbon into one piece 10cm (4in) long and 15 pieces about 30cm (12in) long. Cut three of the long pieces in half. Mark on the opening edges where the six halved ribbons will go; three should be sewn on the wrong side of the overlap, and the other three opposite them, on the right side of the underlap. Also mark the position of fabric ties at the bottom edge and halfway up each cane on the inside. Finally, mark the position for a loop on the outside, halfway up and about a

third of the way around, so the door flap can be tied back. The 10cm (4in) piece of ribbon will be used for this.

6 Remove the fabric from the canes and sew on the loop and the three pairs of short ribbons at the front. Fold the longer ribbons in half and sew the folded edge of each to the marked positions.

HOPSCOTCH FLOORCLOTH

Along with hoops, marbles, spinning tops, French skipping and leapfrog, hopscotch is one of those children's games that have remained popular for generations. Painting the squares on a floorcloth not only looks good, it also allows the game to be enjoyed in the comfort of one's own playroom. Enlarge the numerals from the templates at the back of the book.

YOU WILL NEED

WHITE CANVAS FABRIC

2.5CM (1IN) WIDE WHITE OR CREAM WEBBING

MATCHING SEWING THREAD

LOW-TACK MASKING TAPE

EMULSION OR ACRYLIC PAINTS IN YELLOW AND THREE OTHER COLOURS

ACRYLIC VARNISH

1 Cut a piece of canvas to the size you require and turn the raw edges to the front. Cover them with webbing to form a border. Machine stitch around all edges to secure.

2 Use masking tape to protect the edging, then paint the whole canvas yellow. Leave to dry thoroughly.

Remove the masking tape and paint the webbing in a contrasting colour.

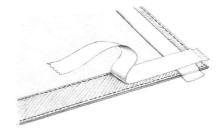

3 Measure and mark out the squares on the canvas. Enlarge the numerals and cut out the shapes from card. Draw around these in the squares.

4 Remove the templates and paint around the number outlines within the squares using three different colours. Leave to dry thoroughly, then varnish.

WORLD MAP TOY CHEST

This unusual découpage toy chest with painted decoration is dual-purpose, being both functional and educational. To make this toy chest, colour photocopies of an antique map of the world were glued onto an old chest with PVA glue. Motifs such as fish and abstract shapes were then cut out of tissue paper, glued onto the maps and painted, allowing the map to partially show through. Finally the chest was given a protective coat of varnish.

PUPPET THEATRE AND PUPPETS

Following a tradition that goes back centuries, this charming puppet theatre is basically just a fabric panel that hangs in a doorway. A window cut into it, embellished with a zigzag pelmet and curtains, creates a stage for puppet shows that will provide hours of fun for children and the rest of the family. Because it hangs in a doorway, there will always be room for the puppeteers to slip behind it and perform. It is also easily portable and can therefore be used in different rooms in the house.

Either use puppets your children already have, or make simple ones from wooden spoons, as shown here. These are ideal for smaller children, who can grip the handles with ease. Encourage youngsters to paint on faces and to stick on hair. Children will also love helping to choose scraps of fabric for the clothes and will no doubt have ideas about colours and the style of clothes. Choose fabrics that reflect the character of the puppet – such as blue and white stripes for a pirate and shiny pink fabric for a princess.

YOU WILL NEED

THEATRE
MAIN FABRIC, FOR THEATRE PANEL
TWO CONTRASTING FABRICS, FOR CURTAINS
AND TIEBACKS
MATCHING SEWING THREAD
2.5CM (1IN) WIDE WEBBING
2 DOWELS
2.5CM (1IN) WIDE WOODEN BATTEN
TENSION ROD, TO FIT IN DOORWAY

PUPPETS
2 LONG WOODEN SPOONS
FABRIC OFFCUTS
MATCHING SEWING THREAD
FELT IN FLESH COLOUR AND YELLOW
2 ELASTIC BANDS
WATER-BASED PAINTS
YARN AND PVA GLUE
YARN

Theatre

1 Measure your doorway and add 15.5cm (6in) to both the width and the length. Cut out one piece of main fabric to these dimensions. Turn under 1.25cm (½in) and then 6.5cm (2½in) on both sides. Press and stitch.

2 Make a casing at the bottom by turning under 1.25cm (1.2in) and then 6.5cm (2½in), and stitching. Insert a wooden batten into it, cutting the batten to the width of the panel. Make a casing the same size at the top.

3 Cut a square hole in the curtain so that the sides are about 13cm (5in) from the hemmed edges. Make sure that the bottom edge of the window is higher than your children's heads but not so high that they cannot comfortably hold up puppets to it. Also check that it will be as tall as the puppets you will be using.

4 Clip diagonally into the corners for 2cm (¾in), and turn under a 1.5cm (⅝in) hem all around; stitch.

5 Attach a length of webbing to the wrong side of the fabric along the lower edge of the window, stitching along both long edges. Cut one dowel to the window width and insert into the casing formed by the webbing.

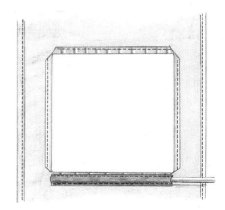

6 Cut two curtains from the contrasting fabric, each the depth of the window plus 14cm (5½in) by the width of the window. Stitch a double 1cm (⅜in) hem on each side and the bottom. At the top, turn under and stitch 6mm (¼in) then 4cm (1½in) to form a casing. Cut the remaining dowel so it is the width of the window plus 7.5cm (3in). Slot it into both casings, gathering the curtains onto it. Using thread loops, attach the dowel to the theatre front, just above the window.

6 Make a miniature zigzag pelmet as for the zigzag edging on page 56 and sew above the curtains.

7 For the tiebacks, cut two 12.5 x 75cm (5 x 30in) strips of another contrasting fabric and stitch together down both ends and the long side, leaving an opening and taking a 6mm (¼in) seam. Trim corners, turn right side out and press. Slipstitch the opening. Tie one around each curtain.

8 Slot the tension rod through the casing at the top of the theatre and fix into a doorway.

Puppets

1 Create two different-sized tunics for each puppet by cutting circles from the fabric offcuts. Cut a smaller circle at the centre point of the circle.

2 Cut four felt arm shapes for each puppet. Glue the arm shapes together in pairs and glue these arms onto the sides of each spoon. Paint a face on the concave side of each wooden spoon.

3 Using a double length of thread, hand sew gathering stitches around the central holes in each circle. Wrap an elastic band several times around the neck of the wooden spoon. Fit the tunic over the spoon and pull up the gathers to make a snug fit.

4 Tie scarves made from strips of fabric around the puppets' necks. For the hat, cut a piece of felt and twist it into shape. To make the puppet's hair, wrap yarn around a piece of cardboard 30-40 times. Slip the loops off the cardboard, tie them on one side and cut the other side. Glue to the spoon, trimming the ends to shape.

CHAPTER EIGHT

Children's Bathrooms

A bathroom solely devoted to children may sound like an unnecessary luxury, but in fact any bathroom that children will gravitate to without fuss at the end of a busy day makes good sense, as it is a treat for everyone. An inspiring and innovative theme to stimulate young ones' imaginations, combined with cheerful accessories and bath toys, will guarantee a calmer, more relaxed pre-bedtime for all concerned.

A separate space for the younger generation can often be devised with a little ingenuity. This will be particularly useful in larger families or where everyone needs to use the bathroom at the same time in the morning.

A child's bathroom need not include a bath or shower; even just a WC, sink, mirror and small storage area fitted into, say, a small loft space, or under the stairs off the hallway, will help reduce morning traffic in the main bathroom.

Make sure that all safety requirements are met, and never leave very young children unattended in the bathroom, even if they are with older siblings.

Bathtime is bound to be fun in a room such as our Deep Blue Sea Bathroom (page 122) inhabited by myriads of deep-sea creatures. Bathed, cleaned and dried amid an ocean scene, children will hopefully respond to the inspired decoration by peacefully complying with bedtime routines.

DECORATING

Even tiny spaces can be jollied up with bright fabric tie-blinds, delicate lace panels or striped curtains in seaside colours. Deckchair canvas and traditional ticking are both ideal for a much-used bathroom as they not only look good but are tough and durable. Try making simple blinds with them and attach them to the wall with chandler's rope. Painted height charts and fun laundry baskets also brighten up the space.

An underwater theme is obviously highly appropriate for a bathroom and is great fun for children. The Deep Blue Sea Bathroom shown on pages 118–19, which is in fact used by all the family, is based on this. In addition to the ideas for incorporating fishy motifs that are featured in that bathroom there are many other ways to introduce an aquatic element. For storing toys, make string bags look like fishing nets by tying or sewing on small shells, then fill them with tiny metal buckets and spades, plastic ducks and wooden fish for decorative effect. Use green nylon netting to make a wall display, threading through small starfish, sea anemones, wooden sailing boats and flotsam and jetsam. Edge a small wooden wall shelf with wave or fish shapes, and top it with wooden fish or seabirds, shells or novelty sponges.

Another theme that is easy to achieve in a bathroom is the classic combination of wood and wicker against a white backdrop. Painted Lloyd Loom chairs with floral cushions soften an otherwise monochromatic scheme. Wooden slatted blinds at small windows can be softened by the addition of a simple pelmet above them.

Create a Mediterranean feel by painting and distressing wall cupboards and shelves in vivid blues and yellows, and complementing them with colourwashed walls and red, blue and yellow fabrics in bold, painterly stripes or irregular checks. Combine them with brightly painted wooden toys displayed on a small shelf and bathtime will never seem dull.

SURFACE MAGIC

Tiles are the most obvious choice for bathroom walls. If you are putting up new tiles, look for designs and colours that bear out your theme – there are, for example, some lovely fish tiles.

Tongue-and-groove panelling is at once practical and appealing in a bathroom used predominantly by children. Protected with paint and/or varnish, it will withstand spills and also provide a background for a decorative splashback. This can be painted, sponged or stencilled with images that match the style of the room. Top with a narrow, lipped shelf for seashore paraphernalia and children's toiletries.

A splashboard, cut into a wavy shape with a jigsaw and decorated with colourful fish motifs, can be mounted straight onto a wall or, as in our Deep Blue Sea Bathroom (page 122), fixed onto existing tongue-and-groove boarding.

USING MOTIFS

If you feel confident about your painting skills, try painting a freehand frieze or a row of repeating motifs such as seaweed, stars, polkadots or a wavy line. Otherwise, cut out simple shapes from magazines to use as templates for stencils; or photocopy then paint with water-based paint and stick them to the splashback with PVA glue. Seal with varnish to make them waterproof.

Sponging is a supremely easy way of transferring images from one surface to another. Simple images without much detail are best for sponging. Just mark your chosen shape on a thick decorating sponge with a marker pen, cut out the shape using a craft knife, take up some paint then use it to stamp the images. This is simple enough that children can help with it too.

Underwater images can be created by painting freehand, stencilling, sponging or stamping. Let children help so they can sit in the bath and admire their handiwork.

STORAGE

Bathroom cabinets are also very simple to make or decorate. Use a piece of junk shop furniture to create a stylized cupboard decorated with fish and shells, or use rough, old floorboards to make a driftwood-style cabinet, complete with antique door lock, huge metal key and chandler's rope as a door pull. Build in a mirror to the inside of the door, or at the front.

Storing bath toys in a small space calls for a touch of ingenuity. A good solution is to use a dual-purpose container such as a wooden box on castors which can double as a small seat. A strong, lidded wicker chest would serve just as well. Alternatively, freestanding open metal shelves will store towels and toiletries at the top and toys below.

SAFETY CONSIDERATIONS

Safety is important in a children's bathroom. Make sure that the flooring is a non-slip, wipe-clean material such as cork or linoleum. Any rugs should be placed on a non-slip mat or have a non-slip backing. Use a sturdy step for smaller children to reach the sink. Store all medicines in a lockable cabinet, out of reach. See page 130 for more information on bathroom safety.

THE DEEP BLUE SEA BATHROOM

Our children's bathroom (shown on pages 118–19) was inspired by the glorious blues of the ocean and the infinite variety of sea life. Get children to help choose fishy accessories for the bath and appropriate towels. They will feel awfully important when showing friends the way to "their" bathroom.

BATH SPLASHBACK

This splendid underwater scene, applied to painted MDF (medium-density fibreboard) by means of sponge-prints, stencils and freehand painting, is an inspiring backdrop for reluctant bathers. Children can help with the sponging, as it is as simple as potato printing. The motifs, many of which have templates at the back of the book, echo those on the fabric window blind. Screwed onto existing panelling with cross-head screws, a splashback like this can be easily removed for a revamp or a different story.

YOU WILL NEED

MDF (MEDIUM-DENSITY FIBREBOARD)
JIGSAW
EMULSION PAINT IN DEEP BLUE
ACRYLIC PAINTS IN A VARIETY OF COLOURS
SPONGES, STENCILS AND PAINTBRUSHES
MATT ACRYLIC VARNISH

1 Draw wave shapes on the sheets of MDF and cut out the outlines with a jigsaw. Sand the edges smooth. Paint the MDF with emulsion paint in deep blue for the background.

2 Apply the fish and plant motifs by a variety of methods. Cut fish shapes from sponges and coat these with a thin layer of acrylic paint. Stencil some motifs in one or two colours, using brushes or sponges to apply the paint through the stencil. Detailing such as eyes can be hand-painted, and you can also paint whole motifs freehand if you wish.

3 Apply a couple of coats of matt acrylic varnish to protect the surface, allowing it to dry between coats.

TROPICAL FISH CABINET

Painted decoration transforms an old junk shop cupboard into a children's bathroom cabinet that is both fanciful and functional. The contrasting textures of the distressed surface, the background colours and the tropical fish and shells all add to its appeal.

The cabinet has been decorated using diluted emulsion paints for a faded, watery finish, though the uneven, rough texture of the background is achieved by painting the diluted water-based paint over an oil base in a deeper colour. The waves and bubbles are added with diluted white emulsion paint. The distinctive translucency and texture of the tropical fish and shells are created by gluing tissue paper shapes onto the cabinet with PVA glue and then painting them. Finally, the cabinet is varnished to protect it from the watery environment.

PAINTED DECORATION

Panelled doors and wooden bathroom furniture offer surfaces tailormade for underwater motifs. For this cupboard door, pale blue water-based paint was diluted to produce a washy texture and broken surface. The orange fish were created by cutting out sponge shapes and coating them with a layer of orange paint before stamping them on rather like potato prints. The purple fish were applied using a stencil. Finally, the decoration was sealed with a matt acrylic varnish. The table was painted with a wave-motif edging to echo the splashback.

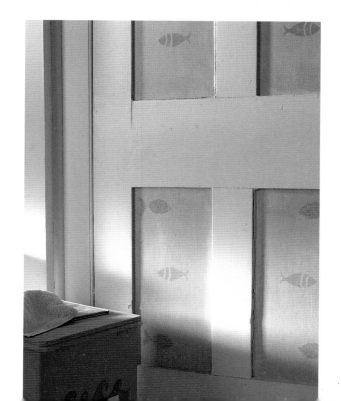

HEIGHT CHART

Children love checking how much they have grown, and a height chart on the bathroom wall is a splendid way to involve them in decorating the room. This one has been painted onto a strip of plain lining paper trimmed to fit the tongue-and-groove boarding, but you could mount the painted paper on a plain wall, or paint straight onto panelling. The painting technique and motifs are the same as for the Bath Splashback (see page 122), with each measurement painted onto a bubble.

DRAWSTRING BAGS

Fabric bags hanging from hooks provide a handy place to keep children's bathroom paraphernalia. For each bag, cut out a rectangle and fold it in half crosswise, right sides together. Stitch down one side and across the end, leaving a 2cm (¾in) opening in the side seam starting 13cm (5in) from the top. Trim the corners, turn right side out and press. Turn under 6mm (¼in) and then 7.5cm (3in) on the top edge and stitch. Stitch again, 4.5cm (1¾in) from the top edge, to form a casing.

Make up a narrow fabric tie by cutting a 4cm (1½in) wide strip of the same fabric, folding the long raw edges to nearly meet at the centre and then folding it in half lengthwise. Press. Stitch down the side and across both ends. Attach a safety pin to one end and insert it through the opening in the side seam. Push it through the casing from the outside, back to the opening. Remove the safety pin, use the tie to draw up the bag and then knot the ends for hanging.

TIE-UP BLIND

This pretty blind will brighten up any window. With its colourful underwater design, the fabric is ideal for children's bathrooms and was the source of inspiration for the fish decoration used elsewhere in our Deep Blue Sea Bathroom.

Backed with a toning dotty material, which is also used for the two pairs of ties that hold the blind up, it provides a cheerful way of blocking either the view or direct sunlight. It is also extremely quick and easy to make.

The blind is simply attached to the top of the window frame (or to a batten on the wall above) with a strip of Velcro. This type of blind is most suited to windows where it won't need to be constantly raised and lowered, and where you do not need totally to block out the light. It is the perfect solution for bathroom windows that are not directly overlooked.

YOU WILL NEED

MAIN FABRIC
BACKING FABRIC
MATCHING SEWING THREAD
SEW-AND-STICK VELCRO

MEASURING

Measure the area you want the blind to cover and add 2.5cm (1in) to the width and 4cm (1½in) to the length for seams. The two pairs of ties will need to be this length plus extra for tying into bows.

1 Cut out a rectangle to the correct dimensions from the main fabric, and another from the backing fabric. Cut out four fabric strips for the ties, each to the desired length by a width of 11.5cm (4½in).

2 Fold each long fabric strip in half lengthwise, right sides together and raw edges even, and stitch a 6mm (¼in) seam down the long edge and across one end. Trim off the corners, turn right side out and press.

3 Lay the backing piece right side up on a flat surface. Place two ties on top, one tie over the other, parallel to the long edge of the backing piece and with the unstitched ends even with the raw edge of the fabric. They should be one-quarter of the way in from the edge. Repeat for the other pair of ties,

placing them the same distance in from the opposite edge.

4 Place the main fabric piece on top, right side down, sandwiching the ties in between. Stitch a 1.25cm (½in) seam around the side and bottom edges, and a 2.5cm (1in) seam at the top edge, leaving an opening in the centre of the top edge. The opening should be about one-third of the total width so it misses the ties.

5 Turn right side out, and press. Turn in the raw edges of the opening, and slipstitch to close. Allow one tie from each piece to hang down the front and the other down the back; tack in place at the top. Stitch the sew-on piece of a strip of Velcro to the top edge. Remove the tacking.

6 Stick the self-adhesive side of the Velcro strip along the top of the window or batten. Roll up the blind by hand to the desired height and tie two nice fat bows to hold it.

BATH MAT

Simple fish shapes are perfect to appliqué onto a plain bath mat. Just cut the shapes out of coloured towelling, turn under a narrow hem around all edges and slipstitch in place on the mat. Instead of towelling, you could use face cloths that match your bath towels.

SAFE AND SOUND

The need to keep your children safe and protected in the home should always be balanced against their need to explore experiences and test their own capabilities.

However, there are many devices and much sensible advice available today which have helped reduce greatly the number of accidents occurring in the home.

KITCHEN

The kitchen is a potentially hazardous room, especially when toddlers are underfoot during food preparation or chores, but a few sensible precautions can prevent serious mishaps.

Where possible, try to keep children and their toys away from the main areas of food preparation and cooking.

Flooring should be kept clean, dry and free of toys that are not being played with and can be too easily tripped over. Do not have any loose rugs in the kitchen, where people move about constantly.

Sufficient worktop lighting is important. Make sure too that a table used for children's activities or homework is well lit from overhead, or with a table lamp if appropriate.

If choosing a new cooker, consider buying an eye-level grill and oven, or a floor-standing oven with a well-insulated door and childproof knobs. Fit a cooker guard around the hob and always turn in saucepan handles when cooking. Use the back rings rather than the front ones.

Always store bleach and other household detergents in a lockable cupboard or high up out of reach. Keep knives and other sharp tools, such as food mixer blades, out of reach.

Do not store glasses or precious china at a low level. Either fit all kitchen cupboards with child-resistant catches or store dangerous items up high and make it clear to your child that they are not allowed to open some cupboards.

Allocate one or two cupboards that are safe for them to open and explore. That way you will probably find they no longer try to discover the contents of the others – unless you leave the doors open. Store safe but interesting items there, such as light saucepans, wooden spoons and empty yoghurt pots, changing the contents slightly now and then so they get a surprise when they return to it. Small cans of food or light plastic food containers would not harm children if they mistakenly opened a low cupboard.

In case of fire, a smoke detector should be fitted nearby (but not actually in the kitchen), and a fire blanket and fire extinguisher should be kept in a safe place in the kitchen.

When electrical appliances such as toasters, electric kettles, mixers, food processors or coffee machines are not in use, be sure to unplug them from the mains. Attach curly leads to kettles to make them less accessible to a child.

LIVING ROOMS

Most accidents in living rooms occur because of poorly guarded fireplaces or unsupervised children falling from furniture.

Avoid placing furniture near a fire, particularly if filled with polyurethane foam. This foam is no longer sold, because of the speed with which it catches fire and the toxic fumes it releases in the process, but it still exists in older furniture. Fireplaces that are used should always be protected with a fireguard that extends to each side of the hearth and can be screwed to the wall to prevent a child removing it.

Coffee tables should have rounded edges and no glass tops. When children are toddlers you may find it easier to move the coffee table out of sight for a while, as they will delight in trying to climb on, over and under it at any opportunity. Use table corner protectors for any sharp, low-level shelves or units.

On wooden floors, make sure that rugs are fitted with a non-slip underlay and that any varnish or floor polish does not make the floor unduly slippery. If your children are asthmatic or prone to eczema, wooden floors are better as they retain far less dust than fitted carpets.

Conceal the flexes of freestanding lamps behind pieces of furniture where possible, and fit any unused electrical sockets with safety guards. Use cable clips to avoid trailing flexes behind televisions and video recorders.

Keep all breakables and alcoholic drinks out of reach, on shelves or in cupboards. Bookcases that could be pulled over should be screwed to the wall. Consider fixing alcove shelves higher up the wall for storing precious items.

Glazed doors or French windows should be fitted with safety glass, or the existing glass covered with safety film. Put stickers on large areas of glass to help prevent them from becoming "invisible". Casement windows should be fitted with locks to prevent small children from opening them and possibly even climbing through them. (Be sure to keep the keys nearby in case of fire.)

CHILDREN'S ROOMS

In the nursery, temperature control is very important, particularly during the winter months. Very tiny babies, under three months old, are unable to regulate their own body temperatures, so it is vital that the room is kept at a constant temperature during the first few weeks, ideally around 19-22 degrees Celsius (65-73 degrees Fahrenheit).

Do not place a cot too near a door or window where your baby could be exposed to draughts.

Ensure that the cot conforms to safety regulations, with bars no less than 2.5cm (1in) and no more than 6cm (2½in) apart. Make sure that cot bumpers have only short ties so there is no danger of their becoming entwined around your baby's neck or of your baby swallowing one. Never give a baby under one year old a pillow, in either a pram, Moses basket or cot.

A baby alarm will give you peace of mind if the layout of your house tends to muffle the sound of a baby's crying.

Fit a dimmer switch to the overhead light in the nursery so you can check on your baby without disturbing him or her when you go to bed.

Nappy changing should be carried out on a flat, stable surface. A changing mat on the floor is the safest place, but this can give you backache, so you might decide to use a changing table or chest of drawers placed against a wall. A table or chest should ideally have a rim around the edge to help prevent the baby from falling

off. Never leave your baby unattended on any of these surfaces. Always finish changing a nappy before answering the doorbell, the telephone or a demanding toddler.

As your child grows and needs a bed you have various options open to you. Raised beds and bunk beds are great for children over five years old. A single bed can be protected with a guard on the side to ensure that a two- or three-year-old does not fall out at night.

Use only small chests of drawers or bookcases screwed to the wall so they can't be pulled over.

Keep nappies, nappy cream, nappy buckets and sterilizing fluid out of reach of toddlers, in a lockable cupboard.

BATHROOMS

When children are around, try to keep all potentially dangerous bathroom chemicals, medicines, tablets, razor blades and razors, cosmetics and so on in one place, ideally in a wall-mounted, lockable cabinet that is out of reach of the WC and bath area. Children could otherwise climb onto the toilet to gain access if it was left unlocked at any time.

Place a non-slip mat in the bath so babies and toddlers do not slide around too much at bathtime. If a shower has a glass screen or door, make sure it is made of safety glass.

Check that all light switches are either located outside the bathroom or are operated according to local safety regulations, which vary from country to country.

HALLS AND STAIRS

Halls and stairways should have adequate lighting so that everyone can climb the stairs safely at night. If you don't like to leave the landing light on all night, at least fit a plug-in safety night light. Use a safety gate at the bottom

and top of the stairs until your child can safely go up and come down backwards.

Check that your front door has an additional catch high up – either a chain or a bolt – so that children cannot suddenly run out onto the road.

GENERAL SAFETY

Fit a smoke detector in the nursery and check the batteries regularly.

When painting and decorating a child's room, bear in mind that the solvents in oil-based paints like eggshell and gloss emit pungent vapours during application. Always do any decorating of the nursery well in advance of a baby's arrival and with all windows open, since the fumes take some time to dissipate. Wherever possible, consider using water-based paints such as emulsion instead; they are safer.

Never leave power tools or other decorating implements around, either during or after a decorating task. Stencil paints, scrapers and even sandpaper are all potentially hazardous in the wrong hands.

Make sure that the strings on blinds, as well as curtain pullers and side-winders are knotted up well out of an inquisitive toddler's reach until he or she is old enough to know not to swing on them, play with them or in any other way get tangled up in them!

TEMPLATES (OVERLEAF)

Enlarge the templates on pages 132–9 either by transferring them square by square onto squared paper of the size specified for each template, or by using a photocopier. The templates that are one-third actual size need to be enlarged to 300 per cent, those that are one-half actual size to 200 per cent, and those that are two-thirds actual size to 150 per cent.

TEMPLATES

Owl and the Pussycat Bedroom:
Moon and five-pointed star templates for stencilling tops of walls (page 48) and four-pointed star for design on Four-poster Bed Frame (page 53). These templates are one-third actual size. I square = 10cm (4in).

Ducks Nursery: Large duck templates for Ducks and Flowers Wall Hanging (pages 42-3) and small duck template for stencilling inside cupboard (page 32). These templates are one-third actual size.
I square = 10cm (4in).

132

Amazon Bedroom: Parakeet templates for Tie-top Jungle Curtains (page 64). These templates are two-thirds actual size. 1 square = 5cm (2in).

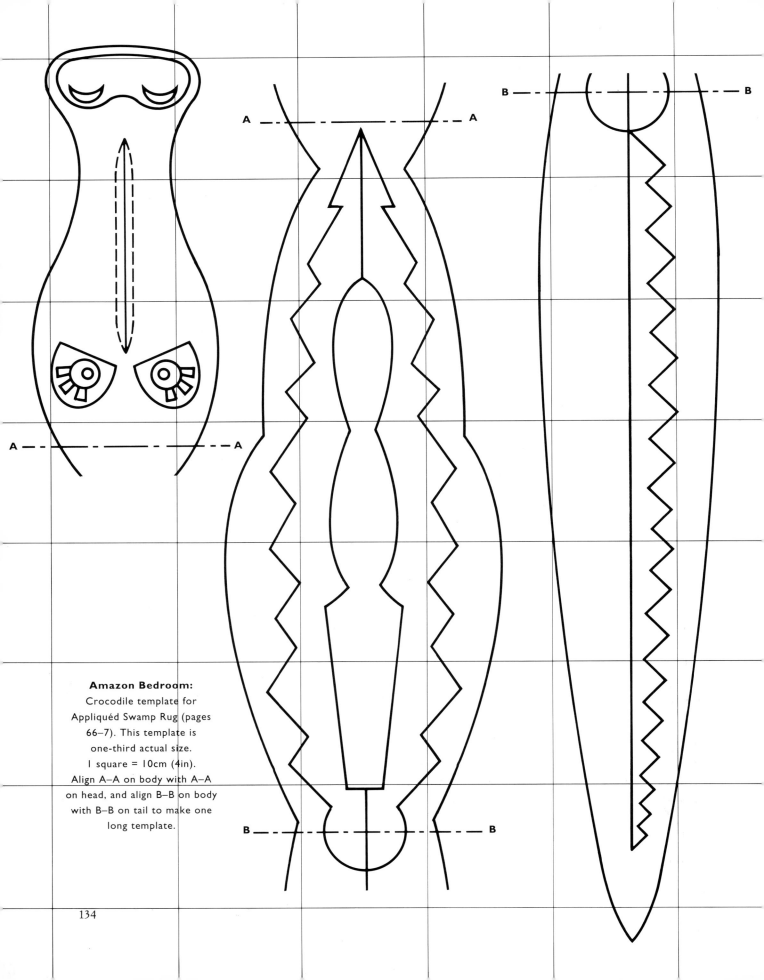

Amazon Bedroom:
Crocodile template for
Appliquéd Swamp Rug (pages
66–7). This template is
one-third actual size.
1 square = 10cm (4in).
Align A–A on body with A–A
on head, and align B–B on body
with B–B on tail to make one
long template.

Amazon Bedroom:
Selection of waterlily templates for
Appliquéd Swamp Rug (pages 66–7). These
templates are one-third actual size.
I square = I0cm (4in).

135

Sailor's Bedroom:
Nautical templates for Customized Flags
(page 76). These templates are two-thirds
actual size. 1 square = 5cm (2in).

Little Princess's Bedroom: Large scroll template for Stencilled Wallpaper Border (page 84) and small scroll template for Painted Decoration (door, page 86). These templates are one-half actual size. 1 square = 5cm (2in).

Creative Play Room: Numerals and alphabet templates for Colour-by-Number Walls (page 110) and Hopscotch Floorcloth (page 106).

These templates are one-third actual size. 1 square = 10cm (4in).

Deep Blue Sea Bathroom:
Underwater life templates for Bath
Splashback, Tropical Fish Cabinet,
Painted Decoration and Height Chart
(pages 122–4). These templates
are two-thirds actual size.
1 square = 5cm (2in).

LAURA ASHLEY SHOPS

UNITED KINGDOM
LONDON SHOPS
Brent Cross 0181 202 2679
Covent Garden 0171 240 1997
Ealing 0181 579 5197
Kensington 0171 938 3751
Knightsbridge (clothes only)
 0171 823 9700
Knightsbridge (home
 furnishings only)
 0171 235 9797
Marble Arch 0171 355 1363
Oxford Circus 0171 437 9760

COUNTRY SHOPS
Aberdeen 01224 625787
Aylesbury 01296 84574
Banbury 01295 271295
Barnet 0181 449 9866
Bath 01225 460341
Bedford 01234 211416
Belfast 01232 233313
Beverley 01482 872444
Birmingham 0121 631 2842
Bishops Stortford
 01279 655613
Bournemouth (clothes only)
 01202 293764
Brighton 01273 205304
Bristol, Broadmead
 0117 922 1011
Bristol, Clifton 0117 927 7468
Bromley 0181 290 6620
Bury St Edmunds
 01284 755658
Cambridge 01223 351378
Canterbury 01227 450961
Cardiff 01222 340808
Carlisle 01228 48810
Chelmsford 01245 359602
Cheltenham 01242 580770
Chester (clothes only)
 01244 313964
Chester (home furnishings only)
 01244 316403
Chichester 01243 775255
Colchester 01206 562692
Derby 01332 361642
Dudley 01384 79730
Eastbourne 01323 411955
Edinburgh (clothes only)
 0131 225 1218
Edinburgh (home furnishings
 only) 0131 225 1121
Epsom 01372 739595

Exeter 01392 53949
Farnham 01252 712812
Gateshead 0191 493 2411
Glasgow 0141 226 5040
Guildford 01483 34152
Harrogate 01423 526799
Hereford 01432 272446
High Wycombe 01494 442394
Hitchin 01462 420445
Horsham 01403 259052
Ipswich 01473 216828
Isle of Man 01624 801213
Jersey 01534 608084
Kings Lynn 01553 768881
Kingston 0181 549 0055
Leamington Spa 01926 314584
Leeds 0113 245 0622
Leicester 01162 513165
Lincoln 01522 511611
Llanidloes 01686 412557
Maidstone 01622 750138
Manchester 0161 834 7335
Middlesbrough 01642 226034
Milton Keynes 01908 660190
Newcastle-Under-Lyme
 01782 662014
Newport I.O.W. 01983 821806
Northampton (clothes only)
 01604 231975
Norwich 01603 632958
Nottingham 01159 503366
Oxford 01865 791689
Perth 01738 623141
Peterborough 01733 311766
Plymouth 01752 268344
Preston 01772 202425
Reading 01734 594313
Richmond 0181 940 9556
Salisbury 01722 338383
Sheffield 0114 270 1855
Sheffield Meadowhall
 0114 256 8221
Shrewsbury 01743 351467
Skipton 01756 700301
Solihull 0121 704 4344
Southampton 01703 228944
Southport 01704 546214
St Albans 01727 864611
Stockport 0161 474 7927
Stratford-Upon-Avon
 01789 298852
Sutton 0181 643 9790
Sutton Coldfield
 0121 355 3671
Swindon 01793 641727

Taunton 01823 288202
Tenterden 01580 765188
Torquay 01803 291443
Truro 01872 223019
Tunbridge Wells
 01892 534431
Watford 01923 254411
Wilmslow 01625 535331
Winchester 01962 855716
Windsor (clothes only)
 01753 854345
Windsor (home furnishings
 only) 01753 831456
Worcester 01905 20177
Worthing 01903 205160
Yeovil 01935 79863
York 01904 627707

HOMEBASES
Within Sainsbury's Homebase
 House and Garden Centres
Basildon 01268 584088
Basingstoke 01256 469510
Bath 01225 339293
Blackheath 0181 856 9767
Bradford 01274 611929
Branksome 01202 768311
Brentford 0181 847 2214
Camberley 01276 686227
Cardiff 01222 499675
Catford 0181 461 0606
Chichester 01243 533373
Colchester 01206 869187
Coventry 01203 715901
Crawley 01293 538351
Crayford 01322 558614
Croydon 0181 684 8250
Derby 01332 291260
Enfield 0181 366 2236
Falkirk 01324 631551
Gloucester 01452 526806
Guildford 01483 304115
Harlow 01279 413355
Hatfield 01707 275837
Hedge End 01489 789797
Hull 01482 572434
Ilford 0181 590 0212
Ipswich 01473 721124
Kensington 0171 603 2285
Kingston 0181 949 7861
Leeds 0113 268 5010
Leicester 0116 254 6075
Luton 0582 593445
Maidstone 01622 715400
Milton Keynes 01908 692727

New Southgate 0181 368 1698
Newcastle-Under-Lyme
 01782 711752
Northampton 01604 234143
Norwich 01603 417474
Nottingham 0115 941 3885
Oldbury 0121 544 7333
Orpington 01689 890353
Oxford 01865 747979
Penge 0181 778 4214
Rayleigh Weir 01268 745374
Reading 01734 584572
Richmond 0181 876 2235
Rochester 01634 200088
Romford 01708 730326
Ruislip 0181 841 8858
Sheffield 0174 255 5175
Stockport 0161 474 7489
Swansea 01792 650935
Swindon 01793 487125
Tunbridge Wells
 01892 546646
Wakefield 01924 387011
Waltham Cross 01992 625275
Walthamstow 0181 531 8233
Watford 01923 252075
Wimbledon 0181 946 9802
Worcester 01905 420401
Worle 01934 512628
York 01904 643911

REPUBLIC OF IRELAND
Cork 00 3532 127 4070
Dublin 00 3531 679 5433

**UNITED STATES OF
 AMERICA**
Albany 518 452 4998
Ann Arbor 313 747 6620
Ardmore 610 896 0208
Arlington 703 415 2111
Atlanta-Lenox 404 231 0685
Atlanta-Perimeter
 770 395 6027
Austin 512 451 4036
Bal Harbor 305 864 5628
Beachwood 216 831 7621
Birch Run 517 624 9297
Birmingham 205 985 0090
Bluffton 803 837 2366
Boca Raton 407 368 5622
Boston 617 536 0505
Bridgewater 908 725 3700
Buffalo 716 681 8600
Burlington MA 617 272 4540

Burlington VT 802 658 5006
Carmel-by-the-Sea
　408 624 8095
Central Valley 914 928 4561
Charleston 803 723 3967
Charlotte 704 362 0926
Charlottesville 804 971 7707
Chattanooga 615 855 5496
Chestnut Hill 617 965 7640
Chicago 312 951 8004
Cincinnati 513 793 5535
Columbus 614 224 5057
Corte Madera 415 924 5770
Costa Mesa 714 545 9322
Cranston 401 946 1211
Dallas-Galleria 214 980 9858
Danbury 203 790 5068
Dayton 513 299 9007
Denver-Cherry Creek
　303 322 9401
Des Moines 515 243 8881
Destin 904 654 2626
Edina 612 920 2811
Fairfax 703 352 7960
Farmington 203 521 8967
Fort Lauderdale 305 563 2300
Fort Worth 817 346 4666
Freeport 207 865 3300
Germantown 901 756 7036
Gilroy 408 848 5470
Glendale 818 242 0428
Grand Rapids 616 942 6828
Greenville 302 575 1653
Greenwich 203 661 5678
Grosse Pointe 313 886 6960
Hackensack 201 488 0130
Hingham 617 740 4122
Honolulu 808 942 5200
Houston 713 871 9669
Houston/West Oaks
　713 558 6113
Indianapolis 317 848 9855
Jacksonville 904 358 7548
Jeffersonville 614 948 2016
Kansas City 816 931 0731
King of Prussia 610 354 9137
Knoxville 615 558 6385
Lake Forest 708 615 1405
Lancaster 717 397 7116
Lexington 606 253 1724
Little Rock 501 666 0272
Los Angeles 310 553 0807
Louisville 502 585 2424
Manhasset 516 365 4834
McLean 703 827 0074
Miami 305 233 8911
Milwaukee 114 347 1930
Minnetonka 612 546 4613

Montgomery 205 284 7011
Myrtle Beach 803 236 4244
Nashville 615 383 0131
New Haven 203 782 9436
New Orleans 504 522 9403
New York City/Westside
　212 496 5110
North Bethesda 301 984 3223
Northbrook 708 480 1660
Novi 313 348 9260
Oakbrook 708 572 9195
Oklahoma City 405 848 6252
Omaha 402 390 2085
Orlando 407 351 2785
Osage Beach 314 348 1333
Owings Mills 410 363 2455
Palm Beach 407 832 3188
Palm Beach Gardens
　407 624 5901
Palm Springs 619 322 2099
Palo Alto 415 328 0560
Phoenix 602 956 6043
Pittsburgh 412 367 8881
Pittsburgh 412 621 0735
Pleasanton 510 463 8714
Portland 503 224 0703
Prince William 703 474 3124
Princeton 609 683 4760
Raleigh 919 781 1076
Reading 215 373 5495
Redondo Beach 310 542 4466
Richmond 804 740 1406
Ridgeland 601 957 9063
Rochester 507 287 1073
Sacramento 916 923 5696
Salt Lake City 801 363 8408
San Antonio 512 377 2833
San Diego 619 234 0663
San Diego 619 452 6116
San Francisco 415 788 0190
San Marcos 512 396 5570
Santa Ana 714 834 1211
Santa Barbara 805 682 8878
Santa Clara 408 244 3551
Scarsdale 914 723 8500
Schaumberg 708 619 9110
Seattle 206 343 9637
Secausus 201 863 3066
Short Hills 201 467 5657
Skokie 708 673 6604
Southampton 516 287 2104
Stamford 203 324 1067
Stony Brook 516 689 6622
St Augustine 904 823 9533
St Louis 314 993 4410
Tampa 813 253 2177
Towson 410 825 0362
Troy 810 649 0890

Tulsa 918 749 5001
Walnut Creek 510 947 5920
Westport 203 226 7495
White Plains 914 686 3404
Williamsburg 804 229 0353
Winston Salem 919 760 3733
Winter Park 407 740 8900
Woodbury 516 367 2810
Woodland Hills 818 346 7560
Worthington 614 433 9011

MOTHER AND CHILD
　STORES
Birmingham 205 987 7566
Chestnut Hill 617 965 5687
Denver-Cherry Creek
　303 322 9403
Farmington-Hartford
　203 561 4870
Hackensack-Riverside
　201 342 1222
Houston 713 622 2262
Kansas City 816 931 2810
King of Prussia 610 354 9137
Princeton 609 683 1300
Redondo Beach 310 542 6228
Schaumberg 708 240 1910
Short Hills 201 564 9600
Stamford 203 359 9902
Tulsa 918 749 5001
Walnut Creek 510 947 3932

HOME FURNISHING
　STORES
Alexandria 701 739 2144
Ardmore 215 896 8293
Atlanta 404 842 0102
Boston 617 357 5151
Burlingame 415 344 1774
Costa Mesa 714 545 7927
Kansas City 816 531 8971
New York City 212 735 5000
Ridgewood 201 670 0868
Short Hills 201 912 9150
Washington 202 686 1200

CANADA
Willowdale 416 223 9507
Calgary, Alberta 403 269 4090
London, Ontario 519 434 1703
Montreal 514 284 9225
Ottawa 613 238 4882
Quebec 418 659 6660
Sherway Gardens, Etobicoke
　416 620 7222
Toronto 416 922 7761
Toronto-Yorkdale
　416 256 2040

Vancouver 604 688 8729
Winnipeg 204 943 3093

AUSTRIA
Graz 0316 844398
Innsbruck
　0152 579254/579257
Linz 070 797700
Salzburg 0662 840344
Vienna 01 5129312

BELGIUM
Antwerp 03 2343461
Bruges 050 349059
Brussels (clothes only)
　02 5112813
Brussels (home furnishings
　only) 02 5120447
Gent 092 240819

FRANCE
Paris
94 rue de Rennes
　1 45 48 43 89
95 Avenue Raymond Poincaré
　1 45 01 24 73
261 rue Saint Honoré
　1 42 86 84 13
Galeries Lafayette, 40 bld
　Haussmann
　second floor (clothes only)
　1 42 82 34 56
　fifth floor (home furnishings
　only) 1 42 82 04 11
Au Printemps, 64 bld
　Haussmann
　second floor (clothes only)
　1 42 82 52 10
　seventh floor (home
　furnishings only)
　1 42 82 44 20
Au Printemps, Centre
　Commercial Vélizy
　Avenue de L'Europe, Vélizy,
　Villacoublay
　Niveau 2 (clothes and home
　furnishings) 1 30 70 87 66
Au Printemps, Centre
　Commercial
　Parly 2
　Avenue Charles de Gaulle,
　Le Chesnay
　Niveau 1 (home furnishings
　only) 1 39 54 22 44
　ext. NR 247
　Niveau 2 (clothes only)
　1 39 54 22 44 ext. NR321
Aix-en-Provence 42 27 31 92

Bordeaux 56 44 10 30
Clermont-Ferrand 73 31 22 05
Dijon 80 30 04 44
Lille 20 06 90 06
Lyon 78 37 18 19
Montpellier 67 60 75 75
Nancy 83 35 21 09
Nantes 40 73 17 18
Nice 93 16 06 93
Rouen 35 70 20 02
Strasbourg 88 75 18 90
Toulon 94 21 89 58
Toulouse 61 21 38 85

GERMANY
Augsburg 0821 154021
Berlin (home furnishings only)
 030 8826201
Berlin (clothes only)
 030 8824934
Berlin (Kadewe) 030 2183016
Bielefeld 0521 177188
Bonn 0228 654908
Bremen 0421 170443
Cologne 0221 2580470
Dortmund 0231 141009
Düsseldorf 0211 327000
Essen 0201 200482
Frankfurt 069 288791
Hamburg 040 371173
Hanover 0511 326919
Heidelberg 06 22 1189851
Karlsruhe 0721 25968
Munich 089 2608224
Münster 0251 42272
Nürenberg 0911 2451819
Stuttgart 0711 2261064
Wiesbaden 0611 302086

ITALY
Milan 02 86463532

LUXEMBOURG
Luxembourg 221 320

NETHERLANDS
Amsterdam 020 6228087
Arnhem 026 4430250
Eindhoven 040 2435022
Groningen 050 3185060
The Hague 070 3600540
Maastricht 043 3250972
Rotterdam 010 4148535
Utrecht 030 2313051

SPAIN
Barcelona 93 4125490

SWITZERLAND
Basel 061 2619757
Bern 031 3120696
Geneva (clothes only)
 022 33113494
Geneva (home furnishings only)
 022 33103048
Zurich 01 2211394

ASIA
HONG KONG SHOPS IN
 SHOPS
Sogo 852 2891 1767

JAPAN
Ginza 03 3571 5011
Yagoto 052 836 7086
Kichijoji 0422 21 1203
Jiyugaoka 03 3724 0051
Jiyugaoka G (home furnishings
 only) 03 5701 5471
Yokohama LMP 045 222 5308
Futako Tamagawa
 03 3708 3151
Gifu Melsa 0582 66 3136

Fukuoka Tenjin 092 716 7415
Sapporo Factory 011 207 4031

JAPAN SHOPS IN SHOPS
TOKYO
Mitsukoshi Nihonbashi
 03 3241 5617
Mitsukoshi Ikebukuro
 03 3987 6074
Tokyu 03 3477 3836
Keio Shinjuku 03 3344 0080
Mitsukoshi Ginza
 03 3561 4050
Tobu Ikebukuro 03 3980 0041

REST OF JAPAN
Mitsukoshi Yokohama
 045 323 1683
Saikaya Kawasaki
 044 211 8581
Saikaya Yokosuka
 046 823 1234
Chiba Mitsukoshi
 043 227 4731
Mitsukoshi Bandai
 025 243 6333
Sapporo Tokyu 011 212 2658
Kintetsu Abeno 06 625 2332
Hankyu Umeda 06 365 0793
Kawanishi Hankyu
 0727 56 1622
Mitsukoshi Hiroshima
 082 241 5055
Hiroshima Sogo 082 225 2955
Hakata Izutsuya 092 452 2181
Nagoya Mitsukoshi
 052 252 1838
Matsuzakaya Nagoyecki
 052 565 4339
Seishin Sogo 078 992 1586
Kobe Ilankyu 078 360 7528

Daimaru Kobe 078 333 4079
Tama Sogo 0423 39 2450
Kintetsu Kyoto 075 365 8024
Be Me Machida Daimaru
 0427 24 8174
Sanyo Himeji 0792 23 4792
Tenmaya Fukuyama
 0849 27 2214
Mitsukoshi Matsuyama
 0899 46 4829
Saikaya Fujisawa 0466 27 1111
Matsuzakaya Yokkaichi
 0593 551241
Cita Tokiwa 0975 33 1741
Bon Belta Narita 0476 23 3236
Hamamatsu Matsubishi
 053 452 2941
Kagoshima Mitsukoshi
 0992 39 4635
Saga Tamaya 0952 28 0608
Kintetsu Nara 0742 30 2751
Kokura Izutsuya 093 522 2627
Kyoto Takashimaya
 075 252 7952

SINGAPORE
SHOPS IN SHOPS
Sogo 65 334 1014
Isetan Scotts 65 735 0495

TAIWAN
SHOPS IN SHOPS
Ta-Lee Isetan 886 7 241 8860
Pacific Sogo 886 2 740 9662
Shin Kong Mitsukoshi
 886 2 382 4859

ACKNOWLEDGEMENTS

The author would like to thank the RoSPA (Royal Society for the Prevention of Accidents) and Claire, Robert and Christopher Cooper for their assistance.

The publishers would like to thank Mary Batten, Jemima Dyson, Chris Churchley, Denize Lohan, Linda Bramble, Kerry Skinner and Martin Sherman for their help in the production of this book.

The publishers would also like to thank the following, who kindly loaned props for the photographs: The Conran Shop, tel 0171-589 7401 (bedspread, rug, embroidered cushions, canopy on pp 92-103); Far Away Trading, tel 0171-738 9420 (metal coat and hat hooks, candlesticks, coffee table on pp 92-103); The Holding Company, tel 0171-352 7495 (toy box on p 60, chest on p 115, and towel rail and cabinet on p 123); David Shields, tel 0181-858 3534 or 0171-731 7913 (3D ship picture in bleached wood frame on p 68).

The photographs on pages 3, 7, 8-9, 10, 13, 15, 16, 19, 35 and 37 are from the Laura Ashley Archives. All other photographs are by Lucinda Symons.

INDEX